FOUR-LETTER WORD GAMES

The Psychology of Obscenity

FOUR-LETTER WORD GAMES

The Psychology of Obscenity

by RENATUS HARTOGS, M.D., Ph.D.
with HANS FANTEL

published by
M. EVANS AND COMPANY, INC., New York
and distributed in association with
DELACORTE PRESS, New York

Contents

FOUR-LETTER WORD GAMES

The Psychology of Obscenity

1. Intercourse with Lady Chatterley

When the front page of *The New York Times* on July 22, 1959, carried the news that a United States District Court had liberated *Lady Chatterley's Lover* from the bonds of censorship, I gave the headline no more than a quick glance. The sexual emancipation of our age, I felt, had long passed the point where a sprinkling of four-letter words in an acknowledged literary classic should become a focus of public concern. In lifting the prudish ban, I thought, the court had merely removed the barriers that had already been overrun.

The decision, I realized, had great significance in constitutional law, strengthening freedom of the press and granting greater latitude of expression in the arts. But it hardly occurred to me that the ruling might hold any direct personal meaning for people in my social sphere.

I learned differently the following Saturday night. At a fairly fashionable party in Bellport, Long Island, Lady Chatterley ruled the conversation. Thanks to the federal court, four-letter words had suddenly become legitimate news, and the merits of the Lawrentian vocabulary were ardently debated. Party talk was studded with representative samples.

I recall my amusement at hearing a string of barracks words paraded with a crisp Vassar inflection. In fact, it was mostly the women who kept the talk going. The men, for the most part, seemed subdued. Possibly this reflects a difference in the mean level of sexual emancipation between male and female suburbanities. More likely, some of the men may have felt diffident because they had—at other times in their lives—used such words in circumstances or in company they didn't care to recall in the present setting.

In contrast, a lively gaggle of young women seemed audibly delighted at the turn and tone of the conversation. One splendidly groomed and passably pretty specimen of suburban femininity evidently counted on me as a psychiatrist, to keep cool under deliberate provocation. With a radiant smile she turned toward me and said: "Love is like washing dishes. Lawrence knew that. And he knew that real fucking is like getting high on champagne."

I'm sure she didn't believe a word of it. True, she had correctly and perceptively apostrophized an attitude inherent in the novel, and, as a product of progressive education, she may have intellectually sympathized with an ecstatic philosophy of sensual abandon. But, for her, the real point of the remark was not its literal meaning. Rather, it was the use of the word "fucking" as a sort of toy. Like a child showing off a cap pistol, she was brandishing the word as a challenge.

The word itself could hardly have been new to her. Lawrence surely didn't enlarge the vocabulary of anyone literate enough to read graffiti in public toilets. But the stark locution of such a word had been proscribed by a whole complex of taboos. Now the Law of the Land had bestowed sanction on formerly forbidden language. The mysterious, threatening spell that lay behind the taboo had thus been transformed. For her, the word now became a plaything.

The legal decision gave rise to a by-product that the learned judges surely hadn't foreseen. Four-letter words became chic. Cocktail parties, where flirtation and quasi-sexual pursuit are part of a stylized ritual, served as the principal playground for tossing about these new conversational gambits. With the court backing them, sexually aggressive personality types eagerly availed themselves of their opportunity to live up to the Constitution.

Yet the brazen beachhead established by the four-letter word on the permissive territory of the cocktail party cannot be dismissed as just a smart-alecky fad. Casual cachet alone cannot account for the eager welcome accorded such words in what once was polite society. On the surface, the trend toward verbal vulgarity under middle-class auspices may seem merely another facet of a now rampant freedom of self-expression that has spilled into everyday life from the radical outposts of literature. Yet, as a psychiatrist, I see in these language patterns a significant clue to the psychodynamics of our culture.

It struck me that "dirty talk" of this type was, in essence, a new kind of word game—or rather a new set of rules for the oldest word game in existence. Like all true (*i.e.*, psychologically valid) games, four-letter word-slinging serves a social purpose. It provides a socially acceptable projection surface for repressed motives and instinctual needs. The dirty word becomes the main gambit in this game. It expresses something of a person's secret wishes and images. At the same time, it tests society's reaction, or at least the reaction of the person to whom it is addressed. By this kind of word game (expressing-plus-testing), the person can—at least on the symbolic level—strike a balance between his own needs and the norms and rules of society. This kind of symbolic bargaining is consistent with the basic pattern of gamesmanship in most social adjustments.

The four-letter word game played at the Long Island party—and doubtless in countless similar settings elsewhere—jibes with every aspect of this interpretation. In most cultures, the female, even more than the male, plays a role determined, on one hand, by her own psychosexual needs and, on the other, by social controls. The game then becomes a socially tolerated way of expressing both sides of this equation. Adroitness in playing the game becomes an index of social sophistication, and hence of social status. That's what makes the game chic.

This particular game has been played more or less openly in all cultures, though its forms may have differed at various social levels or historical periods. Fifty years ago, an elegant lady's ploy may have been to seem modest and shy, yet perhaps to shift her eyes sideways or arrange her skirt to creep above the ankle.

Today's fashion has exhausted the decent limits of skirt-hiking. Besides, in a curious cultural shift, we are becoming more ear-conscious than eye-conscious in many aspects of life. During the last thirty years the electronically transmitted word as the predominant medium of mass communication has made us more verbally receptive. Consequently, in the modern version of the game, the coy glance is supplemented by the risqué word. But in its psychological essence the game still reflects the often agonizing ambiguity of our sexual mores.

The four-letter word game allows my Long Island lady to remain physically within accepted bounds while committing symbolic transgressions. Her stylish use of profanity openly violates nothing more than fading conventions of polite discourse; yet by implication it overthrows a broad spectrum of restraints. It signifies the abandonment of social responsibility and—as one clinician puts it—"asserts the instinctual, primitive side of life against all the inhibiting forces of the environment."

In this manner, the quasi-decorous use of profanity in a fashionable context becomes a handy instrument for having one's world both ways. With a judiciously dropped four-letter bon mot we can, in sophisticated circles, be at the same time rebellious and respectable, prim and prurient.

This ambivalence points to the nub of the Chatterley syndrome—the acceptance of formerly taboo language in middle-class speech. For this ambivalence reflects precisely the cultural split within the group itself—torn between the proprieties the middle class has traditionally guarded and the temptation to assume the attitudes and poses of artistic libertinism.

This middle-class value split extends far beyond sexual mores. It includes virtually the whole spectrum of social norms, from international relations to fiscal policy, from art styles to child-rearing. The sexual revolution, so lovingly documented in magazines like *Evergreen Review* or *Playboy,* is indeed in full swing. Yet our perpetual fascination with our wobbly sex mores blinds us to the fact that such changes are but one phase of a total upheaval of values now sweeping the western world. Whether we like it or not, the stage is being set for the emergence of a new society geared to technologic control. A psychiatrist's daily work consists to a large extent in alleviating the mind-breaking stress of this cultural turmoil.

Culture in transition offers fascinating vistas to the broadly oriented observer. Yet, as a psychiatrist, I must always focus my vision through the individual. This does not necessarily limit the scope of my view. After all, all human perception is egocentric: the individual mind is the only lens through which reality can be—if not apprehended—at least inferred. Let us therefore return to Lady Chatterley.

When the Lady meets Mellors, his blunt sex words prepare her for the kind of sexual encounter she had never known before. In accepting and adopting her lover's earthy language, Lady Chatterley establishes a community of attitude with him. He no longer seems alien and intrusive. The potency of his four-letter spells has battered her gates of separateness and infused her with warmly miasmal feelings of mutual identity. This relaxes her to the point where, presumably, her sexual responses live up to Lawrence's fervid prose. Through the natural primitivism of the four-letter word, the over-intellectualized Lady Chatterley comes to terms not merely with her gamey gamekeeper but also with her own body. Psychologically, the process involved here appears to be one of radical ego-regression.

Four-letter words, apparently, proved stronger stuff for Lady Chatterley than for my friend from Long Island. For one, the game became reality; for the other, it was a tease. One might think the difference to be one of intensity—that the liberating, disinhibiting effect of the evocative words (or, conversely, their shock value and repulsion) is greater for persons whose instinctual life has been too tightly shackled. The latter, like Lady Chatterley, would be apt to take the game more seriously.

However, I believe that the significant difference in the game pattern of the two women is not one of intensity. Rather, it is a matter of direction. I have observed that the entire psychodynamic mechanism involved here may aim in one of two opposing directions: toward sublimation or toward stimulation.

It has been clinically documented that in certain contexts—mostly at lower social levels—the "dirty" word serves as titillation. For persons of low literacy, accustomed to extrapolate from word to direct action, four-letter terms conjure up vivid erotic images. Very likely, this was Mellors' own reaction and he was able to induce a response of the same kind in Lady Chatterley. In the jargon of a later day, he got her "tuned in on the same wavelength."

The Long Island lady, by contrast, neither intended nor attained such drastic consequences from her choice of words. The notion of dispensing verbal aphrodisiacs would probably have been distasteful to her. Unlike the elemental Mellors, she conducted her transactions on the symbolic level.

The process that separates "smart" from smut is part of a great perennial puzzle. It leads from the physical to the metaphysical and, along the way, touches the profoundest of philosophic mysteries: the relation of word to reality. That problem has perplexed the keenest thinkers ever since man tried the first of many magic formulas to induce the materialization of word into substance. In our case, it works the other way round.

If symbol can turn into reality through an act of magic, reality can turn into symbol by means of the same mechanism running in reverse. Most dynamic functions—like chemical reactions—can work either way. This capacity for conceptual operations between substance and symbol is mainly what distinguishes the human species from other animals. Word formation is the essence of this uniquely human process.

Since word formation so closely parallels the more complex functions of the mind, psychiatry works primarily through language. Four-letter words, I believe, are particularly significant in terms of personality and culture, and it is curious that so far they have received only scant attention from qualified observers.

Consider for example the word "fuck," which the eminent psychiatrist Leo Stone calls "the principal obscene word in the English language." In someone like Mellors, the symbol-reality gradient associated with such a term runs plainly toward sex in the raw. Yet, when my suburban matron says "fuck," she is, in effect, turning away from physical reality. In its stead, she embraces the verbal surrogate, the word per se. It literally *sounds* more promising to her than an inning in bed with her own or someone else's suburban husband. The blunt, compact monosyllable connotes a lusty vitality, a ribald nonchalance, rarely found among the common varieties of household sex.

In her game, the *word* is operative, not the act. That makes the game more convenient as well as more enticing than the real thing. For an unvarnished act of adultery still lies beyond the realm of socially approved sporting propositions.

Then there's the widely suspected though rarely admitted fact that the extramarital lark often turns out to be an earthbound bird. Its transports simply cannot rise beyond the usual limits of physical response, and many blithe spirits never take flight. The word, by contrast, is unencumbered by such drawbacks. It is now socially safe, yet buoyed by its naughtiness into becoming the free agent of fancy.

Such is the fundamental nature of the four-letter party game. Yet to characterize the process as a form of verbal masturbation would be both unkind and untrue. For the implications reach far beyond sex itself. As we have noted, language grows out of the basic transformation of letting the flesh become word. And in the total phenomenon of language the four-letter word occupies a significant niche —one that has so far remained largely unprobed.

In the broadest sense, obscenity may be defined as the language of anti-value. In the dimensions of the mind, anti-value is to value as in the physical universe antimatter is to matter. They are hostile polarities, and their encounter releases the forces of mutual annihilation. Anti-value is the obverse of the acknowledged good. It is unspeakable in the usual language—which is precisely why a special language must be coined for it.

Anti-value is akin to the church notion of anathema. Its very existence is an obscenity to the orthodox. Any language relating to the unmentionable is by definition obscene. It is significant that the words "devil" and "hell"— though of impeccable biblical registry—were considered unutterable during periods of religious domination of the popular culture.

The four-letter word thus is closely related to the curse. It projects and proclaims a universal theological dilemma: a maddening malignity in the heart of the earth, poisoning the springs of life and withering the vision of the virtuous. Hell is the home of the four-letter word.

Obscenity, in short, may be viewed as the counter-code to whatever orthodoxy prevails. It is a defensible assumption that obscenity is as old as language itself. Language is the chief means of socializing the individual; i.e., subjecting him to group control. And the recalcitrant, self-asserting individual defends himself through the curse —the clandestine or defiant utterance of the counter-code, the obscene spell that focuses his psychic force on the annihilation of his oppressors. Obscenity thus emerges as the natural idiom of rebellion.

It is also safe to assume—and recent anthropologic work supports the assumption—that obscenity is universal. Even in the most primitive tribes, the disaffected assail official taboos through the black magic of forbidden words. The specific forms of obscenity sprout largely as local weeds, varying from country to country, tribe to tribe, class to class, and era to era. Among these many forms, sexuality is the predominant theme, for nearly every form of social organization operates through sexual controls.

To study the obscenities of different historic eras might give us more vivid insights into the real cultural dynamics of those times than do the usual historiographic sources. Unfortunately very little documentation exists which would be useful in such a study. Obscenity is mainly a spoken—and unrecorded—phenomenon. As a defiance of official taboo and a gesture of subversion, it was naturally banned from available archives throughout the period of written history. Only in our own time, thanks to the democratic spread of literacy in Europe and North America, has obscenity seen print. And, as a more recent Supreme Court decision in the case of Ralph Ginzburg indicates, the right to print obscenity is still a highly controversial issue.

Even if we confine our historic observations to the brief span of our own century, a few events dramatically clarify the relation of obscenity to social structure. They bear out the basic surmise that the dirty joke or the juicy expletive has always thumbed some outcast nose at the prevailing establishment.

The clergy has been keenly aware of the anti-authoritarian and basically subversive nature of obscenity and the church has always inveighed against profanity, possibly because it felt its own position threatened by it. As late as 1939, Puritan influence in the United States was still strong enough to cause a major uproar when Clark Gable, in the film version of *Gone With the Wind,* spoke his famous exit line: "Frankly, my dear, I don't give a damn."

This may sound mild enough in an age when Henry Miller and William Burroughs are sold at the corner drugstore, but in 1939 Clark Gable's words caused an influential clergyman to thunder: "If this obscenity is allowed, the very moral fiber of America is in grave jeopardy."

The irony is that the irate clergyman didn't realize that the moral fiber of America was made of just the stuff he was condemning. "A good goddam"—that splendid proclamation of Anglo-Saxon defiance of authority and travail—is a natural expression of stubborn personal independence. And Clark Gable's idiom in the role of Rhett Butler reflects the finest tradition of the English-speaking world.

The secular authorities, throughout history, have also been natural targets for rebellious obscenities. I know of at least one coinage that shows the usually close relation between adverse political conditions and the uses of obscenity. As in many other military societies, the soldiers of the Austro-Hungarian monarchy were often the butt of verbal mudslinging. The word *"Feldwebel,"* designating the rank of corporal, was often addressed to non-military persons as a vaguely obscene insult. Significantly, it carried its pejorative meaning only in the Slavic provinces of the empire, where army garrisons exercised their odious repression on the local populace. Even the name of a favorite dish—*Kaiserschmarrn* (Emperor's Porridge)—was transformed into a term of derogation in those regions, undoubtedly because of the nominal link with the hated Habsburg dynasty.

A special province of obscenity in the socio-political sense is the "dirty name" applied to an ethnic outgroup. Words like "kike" or "goy," "nigger" or "whitey" are true obscenities in a classic sense—maledictions to strip the badge of humanity from a feared or despised person. Besmirching the outgroup by such name-calling marks them as fair game. (The words "fair game" in themselves denote a similarly paradoxical value transformation, for what happens under such conditions is neither a game, nor fair.) Here again obscenity serves as a verbal device to mask an otherwise unpalatable reality.

Similarly, the official German use of the "*Jude*" (Jew) from February 1933 to May 1945 infused the term with a kind of profound spiritual obscenity that conveyed the combined meaning of "abominable vermin" and "enemy of the people." The word apparently invoked some primeval tribal taboo. It was partly this language transformation —the deliberate act of making an obscenity out of the name of a people—that prepared the way for the slaughter. Law alone could not have accomplished the dehumanization of Jews in German eyes. It was done by the spell of the poisoned word.

Since obscenity is a creature of time and place, it follows that what is obscene at one time or in one setting may be acceptable or meaningless under different circumstances. Obscenity, it may be said, is largely in the ear of the beholder.

Whether they aim at sex, tribal taboo, religious or political oppression, or simply at outrageous circumstance, all forms of obscenity have one thing in common: they are the mask of fear. They camouflage a reality too unbearable without the release obtained through the therapeutic four-letter word. Obscenity flings contempt at whatever enslaves us. It covers up our doubt and insecurity and "solves" our problems through symbolic aggression.

Because the mask hides our fears from ourselves, the obscene person rarely knows just what he is masking. The freedom he gains through his vernacular is illusory. And often this illusion separates him from objective reality to the point where he needs psychiatric care. The junior executive who mutters about "shoving that memo right up somebody's ass" may merely be letting off steam in a healthy catharsis. On the other hand, he may be building a delusional pattern of vengeful omnipotence against his superiors at the office. Where such behavior begins to attract notice, the psychiatrist can often help the patient identify his hidden fears so they can be faced directly rather than through the mask of obscenity.

My own psychiatric experience with many and varied forms of obscenity has convinced me that it is indeed a sub-language which, however primitive, reveals important and still mostly unexplored areas of the personality and its interaction with the surrounding culture.

2. The Swearing American

The essential American situation is a flat tire.

I'm not altogether prepared to defend such a preposterous statement, but it contains a measure of metaphoric truth. Granted, any attempt to bring a broad human spectrum into a single focus is, at best, an absurd literary device. But I believe that the flat tire, as a gestalt, comprises many salient factors in American life.

For one thing, there is the dominant aspect of mobility, implying a striving toward as-yet-unattained destinations. Equally significant is the fact that—at least for the nonce—progress in any direction is thwarted. Secondly, the theme of mechanization predominates our metaphor, as it does American reality: the machine challenges man's supremacy. Finally, the situation calls upon the stranded motorist to extricate himself from his travail by the traditionally American virtues of know-how and self-reliance.

Such were my musings on a hot day in the summer of 1940, on the highway near Smithtown, Long Island. I had arrived in the United States only a short time before and was busily forging philosophies concerning my new country—a habit common among speculatively inclined immigrants. While my thoughts may seem rather abstract, the situation evoking them was real enough. My ramshackle Nash had picked up a nail in its right front tire and stubbornly resisted my sweaty efforts to put on the spare.

A mechanic summoned from a nearby phone had no better luck. Losing his composure in the course of a futile assault on a rusty hub nut, he exclaimed: "I can't get this fucking wheel off!"

I was astounded. At the time I was sufficiently new to the English language to take everything being said quite literally, and the idea of a wheel engaging in sexual intercourse perplexed me.

In my former languages, German, French, and Dutch, it is simply unthinkable to ascribe sexual activity to inanimate objects. Certainly, these languages have their own rich repertoire of epithets and expletives; but their derivation, for the most part, is religious or scatological. Things may be "shitty" (cf. the ubiquitous French *"merde"* or the Germanic in *"Dreck"*), and, of course, they may be goddamned. But only in America, it seems, are objects invested—at least linguistically—with a lively and rather rambunctious sexuality.

The "fucking wheel" and its numberless analogues are fundamentally different from whatever sexuality is accorded to objects in European semantics. The difference, I believe, lies partly in the fact that common nouns in English have no gender. It also stems from the intensified sexual imagination characteristic of many Americans—reacting against the Puritan tradition. Both these factors seem to have shaped the style of American obscenity.

Having spent many years speaking German, a gendered language, I know from personal experience that the gender associated with common objects often sets the emotional aura these objects assume in the mind. I remember that during my student years in Germany I had a horror of doors being slammed. In retrospect, I believe that this was because *"die Tür"* was feminine in German (as *"la porte"* is in French), and rough handling of such an object was —symbolically—a transgression against its femininity.

To a sensitive young man, everything feminine is delicate and mysterious and not meant to be handled roughly. (Lucky boys retain some of this attitude in later life.) At any rate, it is not unlikely that I linked the gender of German doors with that of living feminine beings, and subconsciously interpreted door-slamming as a threat to my mother.

Later in life, having become aware of the significance of grammatical gender, I often mused on the fact that the moon is feminine in Romance languages while it is masculine in the Germanic ones. Could it be that the less ardent Nordics preferred the thought of a sturdy male drinking chum, a trusty comrade, or a reliable guard as a nighttime companion to the more femininely enticing implications of Luna?

These observations point to the semantics of obscenity in English, as contrasted to many of the continental languages. Inanimate objects in English, having no gender, are deprived of the quasi-sexual associations which grammatical gender implies. American obcenities largely compensate for this lack.

The swearing American liberally infuses sex into the

neuter object. With characteristic extravagance and over-generosity of feeling, Americans tend to over compensate. They turn grammatical lack of gender into a veritable linguistic sex orgy.

The sexualization of inanimate objects has, of course, been widely exploited in advertising. Marketplace psychologists use their persuasive wiles to make cars the country's predominant sex symbols, and designers are obliged to equip our basic means of transportation with mammary and phallic appendages, often to the detriment of their efficiency and safety.

One year, Detroit envisions darting symbols of male aggressiveness—superpowered for jackrabbit starts signifying instant erection. Next year's models may serve as bulbous reminders that the womb, after all, is the ideal means of transport.

How well the commercial concept-molders have succeeded in creating highly sexed mechano-biologic hybrids in our minds seems to be evident from an erstwhile television series suggestively titled "My Mother the Car."

It is natural for a pioneering society to rely on technology in dealing with challenges and changes produced by its own dynamism. Historically, therefore, American men tend to be more involved with gadgets than with women. Many of them still find it easier to relate to things than to people. Consequently, the American male often regards women as things. That way they fit more easily into his emotional frame of reference. As Marya Mannes observed, "The woman is treated as an object, not a subject—another aspect of the hot-rod car—something to get a charge or kick out of."

The traditional American process of reducing the sexual being to an object has now been thrown in reverse: we also convert objects into sexual beings. Industrial design—at least of consumer goods—might nowadays be defined as the art of sexifying household gadgets.

In the May 1966 issue of *Esquire,* an anonymous writer comments as follows on "the sexiness of things":

"An American dairy is trying to make vanilla ice cream 'sexy' by adding ribbons of pink and blue. A designer of packages speaks of increasing the 'sensual content' of boxes. . . . In 20th-century esthetics, the quality of sex is becoming involved with the products of technology."

The writer declares that contemporary products are designed to provide a *"frisson* of pleasure akin to old-style lust" and that things that improve with age—silver, polished mahogany, good leather—no longer merit consideration. "What the contemporary gentleman requires are items that reflect and inform the 20th-century sexual fantasy: here today, gone tomorrow, potent the while."

All of which would be peripheral to our topic were it not pointing directly at the central fact that Americans—psychologically and in their language—maintain quasi-sexual relations with *things.* It is this aura of mechanical pan-sexuality that enables Americans in a sufficient state of exasperation to attribute "fucking" to just about everything.

While obscenity appears to be universal, each culture has its own patterns of obscenity reflecting its own conflicts and preoccupations. The predominance of sex in the American four-letter language is similarly rooted in the country's cultural history. We have a strongly Puritan tra-

dition in conflict with a unique freedom—a broad repertoire of life-styles unparalleled in other highly developed,
organized societies. Exuberant individualism, exploring all
the varied options of existence, is as much a reality of
American life as is Puritanical restraint. One of the main
functions of obscenity in American life is to serve as an
outlet for the intolerable tension created within the personality by the opposing cultural polarities of Puritan con-
formity and the freewheeling search for the self.

During a brief professional stay in the Bible Belt of
southern Missouri, I conducted a psychiatric interview
with an undergraduate student at a local church-affiliated
college. The young man, one of those exceedingly gentle
and earnest types one often finds in the rural areas of the
Midwest, was troubled and disgusted by his roommate's
constant outbreaks of foul language. "He swears like a
P.K.," he told me.

"A what?"

From the reply to my question I learned that "P.K."
stands for "Preacher's Kid"—child of a churchman. And in
the Bible Belt, where they ought to know, P.K.s have a
reputation for being exceptionally ornery and profane.
Their four-letter word game, it seems, is "Getting Back at
Daddy."

One of my patients once expressed the same compulsion
to me: "If there is a rule, I simply got to break it."

Jean-Paul Sartre called murder the supreme existential
act because, more than anything else, it expresses the complete autonomy of the individual will. Profanity as the
compulsive breaking of taboos is related to that kind of

30

ultimate and absurd freedom. The four-letter word stands for the wanton smashing of icons and idols.

Americans like to think of themselves as intrepid icon smashers, tramplers of outmoded superstitions and professional torchbearers providing general illumination. Yet I suspect that the icon-smashing tendencies of Americans —so clearly reflected in their swearing—are less a masterful striving after truth than a frantic sensualized escape from intolerable stress.

The elements generating the pervasive pressure in American life also have long historic roots. Throw the Puritan tradition into the American caldron together with laissez-faire mercantilism and the competition it implies, and you already have a basic conflict between strict social morality and commercial ruthlessness. Add our naïve view of the social process as a one-way escalator toward bigger, better, and "higher" things—and you wind up with the basic ingredients for the current stew in the U.S. pressure cooker.

No aspect of life remains unaffected. Heat must be generated on all fronts to keep the steam up. Journalism, our public voice, must proclaim new crises in every edition. Each board of directors must top the last earnings statement. Soap salesmen clamber after quotas; television dramatists pursue ratings; and our team has just got to beat Pumpkin U. at the homecoming game.

Competitive heat may well be the atmosphere of progress—at least as we define it. But the inherent tension determines the typical modes of American obscenity. It is this tension that also sets a characteristic social atmosphere comprising hard drink and low language at every social level.

In a culture as complex as ours, many other elements enter in. But the overall pattern is one in which the majority of persons, in many aspects of their lives, are constantly haunted by fear of failure. Obscenity helps deny this fear. To the outwardly successful, obscenity is a way of reassuring themselves of their superiority, of showing to themselves and to others that they are secure enough to get away with it. And to the casualties of the competitive struggle, obscenity is a consolation. For in an achievement-oriented society, the curse is the last resort of the non-achiever. As the language of the negative, muttered imprecations become the anthem of failure.

Aside from rebellion against Puritan taboos and reaction to competitive pressure, a third factor has recently added a distinctive color to the spectrum of American obscenity. It is the use of four-letter words as tokens of social equality.

Class barriers in the United States, some historians claim, have become more rigid since the vanishing of the western frontier. Others marshal their statistics to prove that, on the contrary, social mobility is greater than ever in the Land of the Free. In any case, we seem more painfully conscious of social rank nowadays. In the nineteenth century, presumably, such differences were taken for granted and gave fewer twinges of guilt at either end of the social ladder.

Anyone relishing a position of social superiority today must do it surreptitiously. Outwardly, he must strive to be "one of the boys." The curious ethics of our society de-

mand a show of equality while it is tacitly understood
that real equality does not exist. But at least the American
heart is in the right place, and jovial pretense of com-
monness is the new dictate of democratic bon ton. In this
context, swearing becomes an exercise of Jeffersonian
principles.

Unlike the anti-Puritan and tension-relieving forms of
obscenity, which are mostly sexual, the social-equality
type of swearing is mainly scatological, invoking the
lowest common denominator among men. Brought off in
a casual, tweedy style that minimizes the inherent vulgarity, this is often an effective way to remove the para-
lyzing sting of authority.

I know a copy chief at a major advertising agency who
puts novices in his department at ease by advising them
not to drive themselves too hard. "You can't be creative
all the time," he tells them jovially. "Just work in shits and
farts."

Simply by playing with the initial letters of "fits and
starts" he breaks the social barrier between the executive
and the rank employee. "It never fails," he tells me. "I can
just see them relax and mark me down as an all-right guy."

The social underdog, paradoxically, has the upper hand
and the last word in this particular word game. He can
always pull down his superiors by some ungracious reference to their more basic physical functions. One of my
patients, a staff writer on a magazine, had an editor who
constantly belittled his work. Even when his comments
related to such impersonal matters as paragraphing and
grammar, the editor managed to make his point with an

insufferable air of sheer nastiness. Driven beyond the limit of his tolerance, my patient planted both his arms on the boss's desk, leaned across, and said quietly, "I bet your shit stinks, too."

He was of course summarily fired, which hardly daunted his pleasure at seeing his boss flummoxed beyond all expectations. What interests us here, however, is the particularly apt choice of the obscenity. By striking a scatologic note, the underdog can effectively relate to his otherwise infuriatingly unreachable betters. In terms of shit, all men are indeed equal. The boss's self-exaltation is nullified by his gut. To invoke shit as a social leveler is the obverse of the ancient camaraderie of breaking bread together.

To some degree, this incident reflects a shift in American swearing patterns. The scatological remark that so unsettled my patient's boss was not fundamentally serious. Unlike a curse, it had no really damaging intent. Rather, it was a kind of teasing. This is characteristic of a good deal of current swearing. The shift from cursing to teasing parallels a basic cultural trend of our century: the secularization of values.

Time was when cursing was a serious matter. Even well into our own era, many less sophisticated Americans looked on any curse as a contaminant carrying danger of divine affliction. Even children uttering such words in innocent imitation promptly had their mouths washed out with soap, and I venture that this was done as much for prophylactic as for punitive reasons.

Real fear of a curse still persists in certain areas of American life, especially among adherents of fundamentalist creeds. A colleague of mine who serves as psychiatric counselor at a small college in Kentucky relates a recent incident in which a student grew deeply disturbed simply because another student had damned him.

The student had been taunting the other boy about a spectacularly unsuccessful love affair. At last, the tormented boy turned on him and hissed: "God damn you!"

"Don't use profanity," the student admonished, seizing the chance to add an authoritarian tone to his taunts.

But the other boy quietly replied: "I'm not taking the Lord's name in vain. I'm just asking God to damn you."

When the accursed young man appeared at his counselor's office several weeks later, the effects of the oath were obvious. Worry, headaches, and insomnia assailed him. His guidance counselor suggested that he consult a psychiatrist. The boy's academic work had suffered, too; and his bearing, my colleague told me, was downright pathetic.

My colleague was unable to help him at first. "No man can undo a curse," the student insisted. The psychiatrist was tactful enough to avoid a direct collision with the student's beliefs. That would only have hastened his psychic disintegration. But he finally persuaded him that a curse does not take effect automatically—"like a button you push to make God jump to suit your own purpose." God, he explained, is no man's robot. He would take the curse into consideration, like any other form of prayer. But He would reserve action according to His own infinite wisdom. The psychiatrist advised the boy to see his minister and ask to work out some penance for having taunted the other student. That way, possibly, he would add merit to his own case before God's judgment.

The case of the accursed student suggests an earlier era,

when cursing was an effective tool of social control. Damnation was taken very seriously in Puritan America. Awful and arbitrary powers resided in a bad word. A man could ruin his neighbor with a curse.

In this context, one understands why profanity was proscribed by such strong taboos in the Puritan era. For profanity lay not in the curse itself, but in the wanton misuse of the curse, the irresponsible employment of a powerful totemic weapon.

In contemporary America, that weapon has been defused; the totem has been disenchanted; and rumors reporting the death of God circulate widely. With the hellfire of traditional religion burnt out to ash, the curse has lost its potency, and "damn" has been devalued to a mild expression of emphasis—something like "truly." This enables Rex Harrison to shout "damn" four times in a row when, in *My Fair Lady*, he discovers that he has grown "accustomed to her face." Everyone thinks it's charming; and nobody worries much any more about the Whiffenpoofs, those "gentlemen songsters" who, by their own admission, are "damned from here to eternity." As one of my Harvard colleagues once observed: "That's not really surprising for a bunch of Yale men."

Since damning and cursing, minus divine wrath to back them up, are something like issuing a check without funds to cover it, another species of four-letter currency had to be turned out. Sexual taboos have proved hardier and longer lasting than religious ones. Hence the past fifty years or so have been a gradual shift from the religious curse to the sexual imprecation—in short, a shift from profanity to obscenity.

But cultural change now is overtaking even sexual taboos. Only some twenty years ago, Ernest Hemingway—or his publishers—studded the conversation of assorted Spaniards (in *For Whom the Bell Tolls*) with absurdities, as the novel's character threatened to "obscenity" into the milk of somebody's mother.

Today's novels, as we noted initially, are far more outspoken in print. Yet, even today, the pertinent language of sex finds no place in many standard dictionaries, and many terms remain relegated to special compendia of slang.

Crude as they are, many of these four-letter words have the virtue of simplicity and directness, which certainly cannot be claimed for the pretentious circumlocutions employed in their places. And why these four-letter words should be classified as slang is puzzling indeed.

The hallmark of slang is its transitoriness. Almost by definition, slang is ephemeral, changing swiftly with time and fashion. The basic popular sex terms, by contrast, are among the most enduring words of the language. "Fuck," for example, enjoyed a wide linguistic currency long before Shakespeare, and not until the Puritan influence became dominant after Cromwell's ascent to power did printers hesitate to spell it out.

Even the special slang dictionaries skirt the problem. As late as 1960, Wentworth and Flexner's *Dictionary of American Slang* displayed a laughable listing of "fxxk." Typographic word games of this kind would be merely silly, were they not symptoms of a dangerous repression endemic in western civilization. After all, "fuck" is an honest and necessary word. It has no synonyms, only prudish paraphrases like "making love," "having intercourse," or "being intimate." The lack of a workable sex language deprives our culture of free expression in an area where social and personal values are now being redefined.

The absurdity of this linguistic blind spot is illuminated by Robert Graves in his account of a visit by a duchess to a military field hospital.

"And where were you wounded, my good man?" inquired the duchess as she stopped to chat with one of the casualties.

"I wouldn't know," the soldier replied. "I never learned no Latin."

At this stage in our cultural development, we are experiencing a weakening of sexual taboos that parallels the weakening of religious taboos of a generation or so ago. As a result, four-letter words of all types are increasingly becoming part of the accepted vocabulary, giving us a popular language eminently suited for the expression of value change and value conflict in broad cultural shifts.

True, the edge of these words gets blunted by common use. Even so, they reflect new dimensions of freedom now emerging in American life. Outwardly imposed restrictive mores are waning. One may hope that an essentially self-imposed morality will take their place.

The emergence of a new morality is, of course, a long and complex process which does not affect every social stratum to the same degree. Yet among my patients—especially those from the more enlightened segments of the middle class—I have noted encouraging signs of a change in our psycho-cultural climate. Where many of my patients in earlier years suffered essentially from guilt syndromes arising from their inability to come to terms with the proscriptions and taboos of the surrounding society, a significant percentage of my present patients is relatively free from such a sense of societal oppression. Nowadays their difficulties stem at least in part from an inability to formulate independent individual codes of conduct and values and to establish a suitable self-concept. Formerly patients came to me because they failed in adjusting to prevailing codes. Now they come because they fail in creating new codes. Theirs, I feel, is the nobler failure. And surely, theirs is the more hopeful attempt.

In this context, I cannot grow overly alarmed at the proliferation of four-letter words in literature, on the stage, and in private conversation. Seen in the total context of cultural change, there no longer is any moral issue involved. Neither religion nor sexuality is structured along traditional precepts. Consequently, what was formerly profane and obscene can no longer do any real social harm. Rather than deplore the proliferation of four-letter words in casual usage, I regard it as a rising index of spiritual freedom.

3. A Rotten Way to Be Wounded

Hemingway sounded the keynote. "It was a rotten way to be wounded," exclaimed Jake Barnes, the impotent hero of *The Sun Also Rises*. Had he lost his sight, his hearing, or his hands in battle, there would have been appropriate pity, but none of the curious, chill horror evoked by a man's unsexing. By contrast, our official appraiser of service-incurred disabilities, the Veterans Administration, does not rate this particular loss so dear. A blind or deaf veteran, or one without hands, is entitled to one hundred per cent disability payments, while a veteran impaired in his sexual functions collects, I am told, "considerably less."

Exactly how much? To find out, I called the local V.A. office in New York and asked for the public information department. A pleasant female voice answered and I stated my question. What followed was a rather long silence at the other end which I presumed to be pregnant with two kinds of prudery: 1) the squeamishness of women at any mention of emasculation, and 2) the usual prudery of government agencies when asked to take cognizance of sex.

At long last, there was some clicking on the line and a male voice spoke up: "May I help you sir?" From his tone of studied politeness I inferred that he had already been briefed about the nature of my question. Nevertheless, I repeated it.

"To what degree would the injury entail professional incapacity?"

"That would depend on the victim's profession," I replied with as much logic as flippancy.

"The amount of compensation is commensurate to the degree of vocational disability," the official informed me. And without blinking a vocal eyelash he added: "We also consider the possibilities of vocational retraining."

I wasn't willing to settle for such bureaucratic evasions. "Would you say," I prompted with a leading question, "that sexual disablement rates considerably less payment than other forms of amputation?"

"Considerably," the man agreed. His voice made it clear that the conversation was ended.

The government, as usual, had put economics ahead of psychology. Hemingway was more realistic. He knew what really mattered.

In picking impotence as a principal plot device, Hemingway had a sure thing. He was playing on one of the most fundamental and pervasive of all fears—the fear of losing one's manhood, which carries with it the corollary fear of never fully attaining it.

It is this fear of castration—both physical or symbolic—and the related fear of remaining a sexual runt that motivate the bulk of verbal obscenity.

The basic mechanism is one of masking. Characteristically, castration fears are subconscious, and so, to a person suffering such fear, obscenity serves a double purpose: it becomes the symbolic expression of his anxiety, the symptom of his neurotic pattern, while at the same time it serves to mask his subconscious fears from himself.

The person who habitually uses sexual obscenity fancies himself sexually masterful, while, in fact, he is haunted by sexual fears. Though he may think that his obscenity is an instrument of sexual pursuit, it is often the camouflage for the sexual retreat of at least the subconscious part of his personality.

Obscenity, then, may be a way of dealing with the basic and related fears of castration and impotence—and incest, as well. It is one form of response to the psychic wound shared by virtually all men: the fear of becoming a "mother-fucker" and being castrated as punishment for breaking the primal taboo against incest.

Before exploring some of the many behavioral forms of this basic Oedipal trauma, we should explore the reasons for its universality. Freud stipulates an inescapable rivalry between the male child and his father for the mother's affection. Invariably the child is betrayed.

Prenatally, he can claim the mother's body as his own. Even after birth, breast-feeding and constant fondling leave the infant with the comfortable impression that, in some ultimate sense, he "possesses" the mother. But then a profound crisis develops: weaning. The mother's body is withdrawn from him. Worse yet, the mother gradually turns away from her almost exclusive preoccupation with the new baby to resume her normal obligations toward her husband and her household. The male child then undergoes the fundamental shock that shapes most of his later adjustments to the outside world: he learns that the mother is not his exclusive property—that she does not exist for him alone.

From that moment onward his hopeless, subconscious rivalry with his father begins. And it never ends. Later in life, the struggle and the fear arising from this fundamental rivalry may take many guises: competitiveness, anti-authoritarian rebelliousness, obsessive egotism, or, in an inverse form, abject submission to authority or timidity caused by subconscious fear of punishment.

The weaning trauma also establishes another basic male reaction: a fundamental distrust of women. For in weaning and through the "desertion" of the mother, the boy child experiences for the first time what seems to him the essential unreliability and faithlessness of the female.

But the boy subconsciously continues to long for the comfort of his mother's body, and, being jealous of the father, he fears punishment in the form of castration.

This psychological castration fear is reinforced by a simple anatomic circumstance—our upright gait. Lin Yutang, the Chinese scholar, suggests that our feelings of shame and modesty and their emotional consequences stem mainly from walking on our hind legs. When our primal ancestors first raised themselves up on their hind legs, they found their anatomy awkwardly rearranged. Instead of being properly concealed at the rear beneath the body, their sexual organs were suddenly thrust forward and located centrally as in the frontal aspect of the upright ape or man. Very likely, they also got uncomfortably scratched by branches—a risk avoided by four-footers—which may well have left the earliest ancestors of our species with an acute sense of vulnerability and an anxious predisposition to worry about their genitals. Any man who has ever played football, or boxed with a six-year-old child, will find this Chinese theory altogether plausible.

In addition to this archetypal anxiety about genitals, many boys are further burdened by parental warnings not to play with the penis "or it will fall off." Among the uneducated, this barbaric threat is still common. All this leaves in our culture a residue of nearly universal and almost inescapable castration fears that show up in many guises ranging from the tragic to the ludicrous.

An example of the latter sort was recently given to me by an acquaintance who heads the music department of a large midwestern university. He finds it impossible to recruit tenors for his chorus. Because a deep voice is regarded as a sign of manliness, not one of his students will admit to a range higher than baritone. To save the musical situation, he has to tactfully coax natural tenors to take on tenor parts, all the time reassuring them that they are really baritones.

Curiously, the situation was exactly reversed before the invention of walkie-talkies and field telephones. Military commanders before World War I had a hard time maintaining the order of battle through rather ambiguous bugle calls. High voices, capable of carrying above the din, were therefore prized to relay word messages between command posts and front lines. Consequently, a ringing tenor was then regarded as the surest sign of manly valor.

It now remains to relate these Oedipal fears to the use of obscenity. Significantly, such a relation can be found at almost any age and social level.

The earliest manifestation is among boys in the age group from seven to sixteen. In certain social settings, such boys relieve their Oedipal jealousy and anxiety by using foul language in speaking of their fathers. Quite often the foul language eventually extends to both parents. Normally, the use of such language remains confined within the age group. Sometimes, however, it spills over into general situations.

Chester M., for example, described his mother as "that fuck-rotten whore" and reserved even choicer terms for his father. At the age of eight, Chester had come to my attention at New York City Youth House, where I have been serving as chief psychiatrist for the past seventeen years. One of Chester's teachers referred the boy to me because of his flavorsome language in her classroom.

A bright and responsive boy, Chester soon established the kind of rapport with me that enabled me to probe the underlying causes of his precocious obscenity. The boy's extreme loneliness and despondency followed a clear-cut Oedipal pattern. "She fucks around with my father," he complained of his mother.

What might seem like a normal and happy family situation appeared to Chester as a horrendous betrayal. Though still ignorant of the details of the sex act or its relation to childbearing, the streets of his neighborhood had provided him with language denoting only one kind of physical contact between males and females, along with a clear idea that both the language and the act were highly censurable. He believed, therefore, that his father and mother were conspiring against him—doing things together from which he was excluded and which, to his utter dismay, he knew to be bad. Compounded by his subconscious fear of retaliatory castration, this Oedipal jealousy embroiled Chester in a kind of emotional pressure cooker. Fortunately, it had a safety valve. The very language in which he conceptualized the situation served him as release. In using foul language he accomplished a triple purpose:

1) He punished the mother for being an ally of the father, or, as he saw it, siding with the father against him.

2) At the same time, the open use of forbidden language served notice on the father that Chester was not afraid of him. This helped Chester break through the fear caused by the imagined threat of castration.

3) Through the use of obscene language, the boy proved that he hadn't really been castrated yet. The language itself became a phallic substitute.

Of course, I could not explain these complex psychodynamics to Chester, as I might have to an intelligent adult. Fortunately, no extended explanation or therapy was necessary. In questioning Chester about his feelings for his parents, I gave him the opportunity to recognize and express his anxieties. That alone relieved much of his emotional burden. Though he never developed any cordiality toward his father, he began to accept him as a member of the family rather than as an intruder and usurper of the mother, and from that time on his compulsive use of obscenity subsided.

Obscenity motivated by such Oedipal conflict is quite common among boys in the seven-to-sixteen age group, especially in social settings where they are normally exposed to a certain amount of rough talk. Oddly enough, many boys quite abruptly stop the use of "dirty" words in late adolescence. By that time the boy has gathered enough knowledge of the world to sense that obscenity is not really effective defiance of the father. And with his own biologic maturation completed, he can prove his sexual potency in more direct ways. He then realizes that the use of obscenity in early adolescence was merely a childish way of expressing rage at his own emotional and physical impotence.

At this point, a new phase begins. The youngster adopts a pre-adult mode of behavior, patterned after the ideal adult image of his culture group.

But suppose the boy lives within a culturally deprived group that does not provide him with a "proper" image with which he can identify? Or suppose that in his particular group the hero image is that of the criminal, the predator who breaks all social rules and gets away with it? In such situations, the post-adolescent tends to act out his problems in socially destructive acts, such as vandalism, robbery, and rape.

Criminal acts of this kind are, of course, more frequent in disadvantaged groups than in others. Because such groups often find themselves fundamentally at odds with the bourgeois-dominated power structure, young men from such backgrounds are particularly prone to adopt the ideal of the criminal hero. The fact that they may commit acts of senseless violence does not necessarily indicate serious or lasting emotional disorder. To them, crime represents to a certain extent a rational adjustment to an oppressive order. For them, crime then fills the same need as obscene language did in their younger years: the relief of psychologic tension.

I have come into contact with many youthful criminals of this sort, and the majority of them do not appear in need of extensive and prolonged psychotherapy. What they seem to need is sufficient opportunity to work out and adopt a more satisfactory life pattern in early adulthood—a pattern based on getting a job commensurate with ability, earning a living, dating, courtship, and marriage. When such opportunities are made available, a surprising number of youthful criminals spontaneously abandon their destructive behavior and attain a degree of personal maturity which no longer has any need for either violence or obscenity.

The same youthful syndrome—beginning with obscenity and ending in theft, vandalism, or assault—is sometimes found in boys from so-called good backgrounds. I have noticed, however, that in the case of middle-class boys it usually indicates a far more deep-seated emotional disturbance than in less privileged youngsters. This is an important distinction to keep in mind when assessing the subjective meaning of four-letter words at different social levels.

To the slum kid, obscenity is not an alien idiom. He is surrounded by it on his street, and even his parents may use four-letter words quite casually. Their predisposition to vulgar language may well stem from a sense of helplessness in a world which for reasons beyond their comprehension seems to go against them. This general feeling of frustration may be sharply focused on such hapless objects as a wobbly chair, a stopped-up sink, or a stuck window. In fact, any balky object or situation may precipitate torrents of colorful abuse. In boys from such environments, a penchant for four-letter language does not represent a critical degree of alienation. On the contrary, it represents a sympathetic resonance to their surroundings.

Not so with the middle-class boy. He did not draw such enrichment of his vocabulary from his home soil. His bursts of earthy expletive indicate estrangement. The normative influences in his life have ceased to function. Unlike the slum kid with the same symptoms, the foul-mouthed middle-class boy may be suffering a progressive breakdown of ego boundaries that allows little hope for spontaneous recovery. Interpreted against a middle-class social background, excessive obscenity may well be an early symptom of pre-schizophrenic personality disintegration.

In recent years, it should be noted, class distinctions in the use of four-letter language, as in most other areas, have become less rigid and consequently less reliable as a diagnostic guide. Four-letter invasions of the middle-class vocabulary may no longer signify incipient schizophrenia of the speaker but merely reflect a democratic trend toward the lowest common denominator in language.

Reaction formation to Oedipal castration fears, when such milder outlets as obscenity are interdicted by the hero ideal, sometimes reaches truly horrible dimensions of violence. The history of Charles J. Whitman, the young, married, honor student who shot more than forty persons from the Library Tower at the University of Texas, fits the pattern like a textbook case.

Dr. Maurice D. Healty, staff psychiatrist of the university, who had once been consulted by Whitman, remarked on Whitman's intense hostility toward his father. Dr. Healty notes that "the real precipitating factor for Whitman's initial visit after being on the campus for several years seemed to stem from the separation of his parents some thirty days before the interview. Although there has been gross disharmony through the years, his mother summoned him to Florida (where the parents had made their home) to bring her to Texas and she is now living in Austin, but not with her son and the daughter-in-law."

The report continues: "The youth says that his father has averaged calling every forty-eight hours for several weeks petitioning him to persuade his mother to return to him. He alleges to have no intentions of trying to do that and retains his hostility towards his father.

"The youth lived for the day," reports Dr. Healty, "when he could consider himself a person capable of excelling his father . . . He long ago acknowledged that he had surpassed him in educational fields, but he is seeking that status in virtually all fields of human endeavor . . ."

The situation now emerging nearly parallels that of the Greek drama. Upon leaving the father, the mother seeks the son's protection. In symbolic terms, she becomes available to the son, who can now at last prove his superiority to the father in the basic rivalry of two men for a woman. As the final mark of victory, he must kill the father.

But his path is blocked by a double taboo: incest and patricide. So, instead, he resorts to an action which in the land of the Alamo is still atavistically acceptable: kill everyone in sight.

In a society not far removed in time from lawlessness and vigilantes, shooting it out lends weight to an argument. In the logic of the Southwest, a bullet is a category of proof. So some Texans, to make a point, will die with their boots on. Symbolically, they're dying with their balls on.

Whitman's perch was a tower, which Dr. Healty says is a "mystic symbol" to many students who come to the university mental hygiene clinic. Many years ago, Freud also noted the symbolism of towers for the emotionally disturbed. Quite aside from the ballistic advantages offered by its height, the tower of Whitman's last stand may have reassured him that, no matter what his guilt, he wasn't castrated.

It may seem a long way from the furtively scribbled "fuck" on a privy wall to the carefully planned paramilitary precision of the Texas massacre. Yet, psychologically, the same line of causation extends to them both. It might even be argued that, had Whitman been less of a rigidly organized perfectionist and more content with the casual relief afforded by a curse, he and fifteen others might have survived his troubles.

If our observations on juvenile obscenity and related

symptoms have been so far confined to boys, the reason is simply that the use of four-letter words is much more prevalent among them. Girls, to be sure, have plenty of Oedipal problems, but they are of a different sort and do not impel them toward obscenity through castration fears. Yet there is a brief span in the life of adolescent girls—usually around the age of fifteen—when they huddle together at slumber parties and on similar occasions to compare, between compulsive giggles, their four-letter vocabularies.

One of my colleagues, who has spent a few summers as psychiatric advisor at a girls' camp, remarked that these smut-swapping sessions among young girls make her think of women opening their jewel boxes to show each other their baubles. In a way, learning dirty words to a young girl is rather like acquiring a precious and mysterious ornament—a harbinger of the still unexplored world of sexuality that she will soon enter. Toying with such words among her trusted friends helps the young girl attain an aura of emotional readiness for sexual encounters.

Once a girl has gained a measure of sexual self-confidence—not necessarily through intercourse but simply through accepting her femaleness in normal dating behavior—she rarely feels any further need to exchange four-letter words with her female friends. To most women, the use of obscenity is a passing pre-sexual episode, quite different in cause and purpose from the use of such language by boys. Except in pathologic situations to be discussed later, and in the "fashionable" sense described in Chapter One, women rarely use sexual obscenity at other times.

Men, by contrast, often revert to the use of obscenity in later life. The hero ideal influencing their early twenties soon erodes under the frictions and frustrations of adult life. The fortunate man whose energies are then absorbed constructively on the job, in courtship, and in marriage has no need of obscenity as an emotional release. Yet the man whose ambitions and affections are disappointed often finds in obscenity a pseudo-solution to problems he may keenly feel but only dimly comprehend.

Persons intellectually and emotionally organized on a primitive level are the ones who most frequently seek refuge in the old adolescent fantasy of omnipotence and fearlessness woven around the father-defying symbol of "dirty" words. To primitive and ineffectual men, obscenity then becomes the favored form of self-expression. It represents a kind of aggression, often without a clearly defined object, but nearly always exempt from serious retaliation.

The cowardice inherent in the choice of a safe, if pointless, form of attack reflects the basic ineffectiveness of such personalities. You can find them during late hours gathered in the dingier kind of neighborhood bars in virtually every city, spewing invective at everything and nothing in particular, feeling in their foul grandiloquence that their shaky barstools are the seats of judgment from which they righteously condemn the world.

When faced with marital maladjustment, such men often use foul language to their wives, either to mask their own sexual inadequacies or to punish the wives. Any marriage counselor or social caseworker encounters numberless situations of this sort involving men of low cultural and educational status around the age of thirty.

Among my own patients of this type, I should like to single out the curious case of a man in his late thirties who made a meager living by selling Bibles to Puerto Rican women in the slums of New York. His knowledge of Spanish helped, but so did his blond hair and light-skinned, typically Anglo-Saxon appearance: his dark-skinned customers found him sexually attractive. Of course, when he made his Bible-selling rounds, the husbands were usually away at work.

This way of doing business left him with a tormenting sense of guilt and failure. Besides, his constant sexual exertions on behalf of his customers made him virtually impotent with his own wife. This he felt to be a crucial affront to his manhood, and he projected all his resentments and frustrations onto her in the form of sadistic fantasies in which he bound her, tortured her with lighted matches and cigarettes, and also inflicted damage on her with a knife.

Far from keeping these fantasies secret, he described them vividly to his wife, elaborating on her imagined sufferings in obscenely poetic images. This was the only way in which he could arouse himself to the point of sexual contact with his wife. Throughout their coitus, he continued this brutally obscene monologue.

The wife, quite understandably, dreaded these gruesome encounters; and the man himself would have been better off confining his attention to his customers. But a sort of bitter sexual pride compelled him to bestow on his wife what he grimly considered his duty. He accomplished his purpose in the only way possible to him—with the help of sadistic obscenities—and of course he hated her all the more for it.

He came to consult me at the insistence of the wife, a pleasant, handsome, and competent woman of thirty-six, whose steady work as an executive secretary enabled them to send their seventeen-year-old daughter to college. Unfortunately, the husband's mental state continues to deteriorate into a paranoid schizophrenic pattern presenting some danger that he might some day act out his murderous fantasies. I have warned the wife of this and suggested placing the husband under hospital supervision. But she would not hear of it and has so far remained loyal and hopeful.

In contrast to this tragic case, it should be noted that verbal sadism as a sexual stimulant is not necessarily bitter, cruel, or distasteful. Sometimes it helps overcome inhibitions limiting one's erotic possibilities. An element of aggression is, after all, inherent in male sexuality, and where this element is overly repressed, sexual performance sometimes falls below par. In such situations, a few obscene phrases may provide the needed encouragement.

One patient of mine, a young man newly married, could not muster an erection unless, after mounting his bride, he muttered to himself between his teeth: "Fuck her till her ears fly off!"

As an expression of boundless *joie de vivre*, this is indeed a winged phrase. Nevertheless, the young woman, Anneliese, objected. Far from regarding her husband's little speech as a tribute to her femininity and an invitation to ecstasy, she suspected in her husband a darkly sadistic desire to mutilate her.

When apprised of this circumstance, I felt that Anneliese was perhaps a likelier candidate for therapy than her husband, but after a fairly brief period of treatment, Albert was finally able to consummate his marriage without preliminary reference to flying ears.

Albert's trouble, it turned out, had been an Oedipal attachment to his mother that subconsciously so frightened him that he repressed most forms of phallic sexuality, including penile erection. His lusty phrase—a throwback to carefree adolescent bragging—helped him remind himself that his naked wife wasn't really his mother, the only other woman he had ever seen in a state of nakedness. Basically it meant: "It's okay with this one—full speed ahead." Since Albert was otherwise healthy, uncomplicated, and eager, it did not take long to get his signals uncrossed.

Men of higher social and cultural rank are by no means immune to relapses into adolescent obscenity patterns. The main difference is that among such men this reversal usually occurs later in life. During the early years, when men in poorer social environments have already tasted their share of adult frustration, the better educated are still involved in building their careers and therefore have more constructive outlets for their aggressiveness. But around the age of fifty, even a successful man becomes uncomfortably aware of an unavoidable failure: the lessening of his sexual capacity. Or, what is even more frightening to him, he may feel a growing sexual indifference.

This first inkling of his own sexual waning makes a man wonder if he has ever truly been capable of love—a doubt particularly agonizing to men of a more sensitive nature brought up in environments where the philosophic values of love are constantly extolled. As T.S. Eliot observes in his discerning play *The Cocktail Party*: "To men of a certain type, the suspicion that they are incapable of loving is as disturbing to their self-esteem as, in cruder men, the fear of impotence."

Beset by such doubts, a man may pursue his young secretary to prove once again his manly charm and romantic attractiveness along with—he hopes—his sexual prowess.

Such liaisons rarely work out as rosily as they are imagined, and, by the time the man's wife suspects what goes on, the secretary very likely has left him for a younger swain and prospective husband. His ego, that was to be bolstered, is badly jolted instead, and his self-doubts vastly increased.

To deny these doubts and to rebel against the notion of spending the rest of his life as a sexual has-been, a man's ultimate refuge is in the language that once betokened the biologic promise of youth. In reverting to obscenity, the middle-aged, middle-class male once again surmounts his castration fears. But the aggression implicit in verbal filth is no longer directed against his father—now presumably dead, no longer threatening, and mourned rather than envied. Rather, the four-letter words, once lusty and defiant challenges, become a pathetic lament over the first deep intimation of mortality.

Castration as a punishment for violating the mother, as we have noted, is the principal theme surrounding the whole subject of dirty language. That is why the term "mother-fucker" is to many persons the ultimate obscenity, a word of truly frightening power. No other insult compares with it.

At an army base I once observed a mess-hall quarrel among a number of enlisted men. Words like cock-sucker and cunt-lapper flew back and forth without imminent danger of mayhem. But then one of the men said it—softly but with slow emphasis: "mother-fucker."

The ancient power of curses was never more clearly revealed. Icy silence replaced the noise of the quarrel. The colored corporal to whom the word had been addressed froze into a kind of crouch, his eyes fixed, and his mouth hanging open. He was ready to kill, and he undoubtedly would have done so if two other soldiers hadn't jumped him from the back and pulled him to the floor.

It is significant that the man so profoundly moved by this single word was a Negro; for the effect of the word varies greatly among different ethnic groups. Among North Europeans or among Americans descended from North Europeans, the notion of mother-fucking is simply taken as a rather grotesque but basically harmless joke. For the North European, who matures relatively late and who is rarely obliged by sheer poverty to share his mother's bed, the word holds no terror. Hence it does not function as a bait.

Not so among the groups which, in this country, are

spoken of as "minorities"—Negroes, South Europeans, people from the Caribbean area. Because of housing shortages and poverty, families of these groups often live in crowded quarters where bed-sharing between mother and son sometimes continues into school age. This is especially true in certain Negro slum settings where the role of the adult male is chiefly that of a drone who fertilizes the female but performs no social functions as father.

A boy growing up in such an environment is typically confused about his own sexual wishes concerning the mother, especially since a culturally deprived environment does not provide the young boy with social contacts outside the immediate family until he is old enough to join a gang. His entire affective energy thus becomes focused on the often overtly seductive mother, intensifying his subconscious fear of trespassing the incestual taboo. The presence of sisters in such a family and the close physical proximity makes the sexual awareness of the young male even more agonized.

Mothers in such settings are sometimes polyandrous, with a sequence of men "taking over" the mother and perhaps assuming temporary father roles to prior children while begetting new offspring. This adds yet another Oedipal burden upon the young male child: the fear that the mother is essentially unfaithful to him by submitting sexually to other men. Instead of having to cope with jealousy of one father, such boys must emotionally come to terms with a whole string of "fathers"—a truly prodigious psychological demand.

Here, then, is the situation that loads the term "mother-fucker" with its explosive charge. To a man from a deprived social group, the word carries a triple threat: 1) your mother is the object of your sexual attention; 2) your mother is a prostitute; 3) you are, in fact, a mother-fucker. Given the emotional background outlined before, it is not surprising that this word alone becomes for certain men the unfailing trigger to violence.

Hearing this term such a man instantly re-experiences the terror every child feels when the basic stability of the family is cast in doubt. The imagined loss of the mother fills him with a sense of utter helplessness, of being left totally without resources.

The total emotional structure of the man re-echoes once more that fundamental childhood catastrophe of weaning —the searing knowledge that the mother does not really belong to him.

So strong is the emotional dread surrounding the term "mother-fucker" that it is usually pronounced in its entirety only by persons relatively exempt from its effects. Men in whom Oedipal fears predominate usually say only "your mother" (pronounced "ya mudder") when invoking the spell. (Or, in Spanish, "su madre.") The meaning, however, is clearly understood.

A curious parallel exists between this type of linguistic discretion and the ancient Hebrew injunction against pronouncing the name of Jehovah, substituting the Hebrew word for "Lord." In either case, the power of the word alone is considered so awesome that it can be uttered only in circumlocution. Fear, and the resultant repression, extend beyond concepts to the words themselves. What we permit ourselves to speak—and thus to think—is severely circumscribed. Indeed, one wonders what power rationality can attain in human affairs as long as the mechanism of thought and concept formation is so closely geared to unspoken and unsuspected fear.

While the term "mother-fucker" itself has its main currency among the lower classes, the emotional aura surrounding it is beginning to extend more and more into the middle class.

The procession of temporary "fathers" through the mother-dominated, underprivileged household lately finds a parallel in the upper middle class, where the same pattern now gains ground under the polite name of serial monogamy. Economically, the main difference is that, while lower-class fathers depart without much ceremony, a similar succession in the upper strata usually involves property settlements and legal skirmishes. This keeps things outwardly tidy, but the emotional trauma to the children is not assuaged by money, visiting rights, or other legal niceties.

Most psychiatrists confirm my impression that Oedipal syndromes have greatly increased in middle-class families because the bonds of marriage are now more lightly regarded than in previous decades.

New frankness in treating extramarital relations may be salutary as far as the adults involved are concerned, but it bolsters the notion of female faithlessness and unreliability in male children. Divorces, of course, have a similar effect.

Such insecurities are especially pronounced in families

where the mother combines marriage with a career. The career woman's children must share her not merely with the father (or other men who might enter the scene) but also with the demands of her profession. I have observed that children from such backgrounds are prone to highly intensified anxieties throughout life—all the more so since the job obligations of the mother are incomprehensible to a young boy and therefore even more frightening than the natural rivalry of the father.

The man whose mother proved essentially unreliable may feel that, when it comes to truly profound and binding loyalties, no woman can be trusted. This is the man who, even when married, basically prefers male company. Typically, he neglects his wife to attend the corner bar, the Rotary meeting, or that out-of-town conference, finding countless excuses to avoid her company. Contact with her, or any other woman, is at best peripheral.

Often men of this type, among themselves, resort to rough language in a joking way, thus masking from each other, and from themselves, their subconscious fear that they may have homosexual leanings.

The key phrase related to this emotional pattern is "fuck you." If one man "tells off" another with these words, it is neither an order, nor an invitation. But there are certain seductive overtones. I have observed an alteration between two taxi drivers in which the phrase was used on both sides with a certain tender coyness, disguising and displacing a latent homosexual rapport; by verbalizing the "fuck you" idea both men exorcised the taboo, which then ceased to be a threat.

A medical colleague of mine once served as ship's surgeon on a submarine—an environment in which fears of violating the taboo against homosexuality become especially acute. He confirms that among certain types of men the almost incessant use of four-letter words serves as a shield against homosexual temptation.

The very grammar of the phrase "fuck yourself" mirrors the psychology of the homosexual. The reflexive construction of the verb represents the basically narcissistic nature of the homosexual relationship. What the homosexual craves—a love relationship with his own person—is physically impossible at the present stage of human evolution. So he settles for the next best thing—the homosexual relation, which permits him to fuck his own image.

My psychiatric contacts with homosexuals have convinced me that many such persons—both men and women —seek in their partners a mirror-image of themselves. Many homosexual couples indeed resemble each other physically as well as in their emotional structure. Where the couples are physically dissimilar—one representing the male, the other the female prototype—the chosen partner represents an improved or desired, yet unattainable self. Ultimately, each partner seeks to find and love himself.

Psychologically, the principle of fucking oneself, as expressed in the homosexual relationship, is fundamentally different from the entirely autoerotic practice of masturbation. For masturbation is usually heterosexual in nature, serving as a substitute when normal intercourse is inconvenient, feared, or unavailable. By contrast, the drive toward "fucking oneself" seems to be linked to an atavistic archetype harking back through the long ranks of evolution to our hermaphroditic ancestors, who were physically capable of literally fucking themselves. Whoever longs for emotional self-sufficiency as an effective defense against the emotional challenges of the environment may find the self-contained sex life of such creatures as the earthworm or the snail quite idyllic.

The average man enjoining another to "fuck himself" may not be consciously aware of these evolutionary implications, but, at some level of his unconscious, he may sense this biologic truth: by invoking the hermaphroditic practice, he not only taunts his adversary with homosexual suggestions but also relegates him to the customs of worms —indeed a low level of existence.

4. Listen, Lousy (As if saying "I love you")

The name of Clifford Odets evokes no more than a nostalgic and rather patronizing smile from a generation of playgoers steeped in the calculated absurdities of Ionesco and Beckett. But some twenty-five years ago, when I first took a serious interest in the American theater, Odets was celebrated as the spokesman of the bittersweet and oh-so-bourgeois leftism of the Roosevelt era.

Early in my professional life I had developed an interest in the psychological implications of the theater—drama, after all, is an exemplary form of catharsis. During a term as a medical student in Berlin in the artistically supercharged 1920s I was caught up in the intense, expressionist theater of such playwrights as Ernst Toller, Georg Kaiser, and Berthold Brecht. After such heady fare, Clifford Odets seemed rather tame, but he epitomized the American scene in his period. While Germany at that time, confused and bereft of its national identity, needed and created a bold theater of ideas, America wanted from its theater merely gentle assurance that things would get better by and by. For though America also suffered hard times, its national identity had remained intact.

The American trauma of that period was an abrasion while the German trauma was a fracture. Consequently, a different theatrical therapy was called for on this side of the Atlantic, and Odets administered it. He was the man who made the American theater speak the plain and hopeful language of the New Deal.

Last summer I happened to skim once again through Odets' *Awake and Sing,* when one phrase immediately struck me because of its relevance to this book. It illuminated a vital aspect of verbal obscenity: the fact that four-letter words often express a basic sexual ambivalence —the mixture of attraction and hostility.

In the first act of the play, Moe Axelrod, a character on the make, advances on Hennie, his ex-girl friend who has since married someone else. He still wants her. Hennie slaps him, but Moe keeps advancing.

His next line reads: "Listen, lousy . . ." And then Odets adds the significant stage direction "(As if saying 'I love you')."

Granted, "lousy," spoken in an affectionate voice, is a mild enough expletive. But through it Odets caught the essence of the love-hate ambivalence inherent in so many forms of sexual expression. He has also touched realistically on the phenomenon that concerns us here directly: the four-letter word as a prelude to or accompaniment of sex.

Moe's trouble is that he can't quite reconcile his notion of "love" with his notion of "fuck." He loves Hennie, all right, but doesn't know how to say that. So he says "lousy," because that—to him—just conveys the "fuck" part. And that's simpler.

Moe is no more muddled than most well-meaning, tolerably well-behaved middle-class males. In a culture where "love" has meant "adore but don't touch" it is difficult for a man to find the proper niche in his mind for the other thing. Often "fuck" is construed as the obverse of love— "touch but don't care."

The pattern stems from the ancient Judeo-Christian ethic which separates the basic idea of love from the basic idea of fuck. True love, after all, was to be spiritual.

During my brief stint as a psychiatric campus counselor I was visited by a young man suffering from numerous conflicts and insecurities, many of which centered on his relations with his fiancée, which were decidedly platonic. When I inquired into his attitudes about premarital sex, he offered the pat answer that had been drilled into him at the Young People's Christian Endeavor meeting of his church.

"Not before marriage," he declared stoutly. "I respect her too much for that."

"And after marriage," I asked, "you will respect her less?"

The young man boggled. Suddenly he realized where he stood: at the chasm between love and lust. Until then, with a strong assist from the surrounding culture, he had kept the two apart. He was by no means sexually naive or inexperienced. But intercourse had been reserved for "other girls," whom, as he put it, he did not "respect."

"Slut" was his favorite term for such girls. To him, it was the password opening the way into the promised land of sex. By devaluating a girl with this four-letter word he was able to make her an object of lust if not of love.

In failing to reconcile love and sex, the young man exemplified a pattern predominant in western civilization. As we shall see later, it is precisely this pattern that in the minds of men links the erotic with the obscene.

In the past—particularly in Europe—this pattern was thoroughly institutionalized and worked quite smoothly within a certain social context. It was more or less traditional for a man of comfortable means to reserve his fondest sentiments for his wife while casting about elsewhere for more sensual amours. Since the wife often followed a similar pattern, this could be considered an equitable arrangement. It certainly kept lust and love neatly in their separate places. Montaigne, with rather unwonted grossness, epitomizes the attitude: "Marrying your mistress," he writes, "is like shitting in your hat before you put it on."

The traditional marriage of convenience was precisely that: convenient. If romantics have denigrated such marriages, they have judged by ideal standards rather than practical ones. Certainly, the traditional pattern provided both legal and emotional fringe benefits that seem very attractive to persons who have foundered on the marital hazards of our own era.

Since the older rules were tacitly understood by both husband and wife, nobody felt aggrieved. Divorces were rare, property remained undivided, and the lines of inheritance unbroken. In an age when most ownership was personal rather than corporate, this in itself meant a great deal. Emotionally, husband and wife felt free to give each other the kind of affection suited to such amicable arrangements, to share each other's lives peacefully and with a minimum of emotional friction. If such a man, on occasion, found himself in bed with his wife, it probably wasn't necessary for him to call her "lousy" or other impolite things to initiate and follow through the sexual action. Passion, with all its dangers, was safely placed somewhere else.

The modern male, by contrast, no longer has the privilege of separating lust and love. Our age demands that the two be combined in a "wholesome relationship." Women expect nowadays to have their emotional bread buttered on both sides. Men can't always manage this. Too long they have been taught to separate love from fuck, and what custom has put asunder few men can join.

Male efforts to cope with the cultural division of love and lust often take grotesque forms. The more extreme sexual aberrations often can be traced to this basic conflict. There is no point in compiling a catalog of all the odd sexual appetites aroused in this way. Our present concern is mainly with language. But a brief excursion into the realm of music may illuminate some aspects of erotic obscenity.

A young music student showed up in my counseling sessions in a state of considerable perplexity. His main sport at college—and he looked at it basically as a sport—had been seduction. His boyish handsomeness and a seemingly ample supply of coeds aided him in his pursuits, and up to a point he had encountered no trouble.

Invariably he adopted a rosily romantic pose in these ventures, which included some achingly tender music by Delius, which he played on his excellent phonograph at bedtime. Characteristically, he favored a selection entitled *The Walk to the Paradise Garden,* a sweetly yearning interlude with melodies arched over haunting chords that can only be described as harmonic heartbreak.

The young man deeply believed in this music. Its trembling quality of withheld fervor represented his romantic ideal. The girls, so to speak, were merely an accompaniment.

The crisis developed when he invited a thoroughly self-possessed girl with different notions about sex to come to his room. Apparently, she took his advances for granted and even seemed to enjoy them but suggested that he take off that "goopy record."

"Don't you like it?" inquired the young man, crestfallen. By dismissing the music the girl had spoiled, for him, the emotional essence of the encounter.

"Let's pick another one," suggested the girl, thumbed through his records and pulled out a disc by de Falla: *El Amor Brujo,* with its *Ritual Fire Dance*—all passion and rhythmic thrust, without a smidgin of tenderness or sentiment.

That's what undid the boy. With its literal heaving and pounding, this was pure fucking music. Granted, fucking was what he was after. But he relied on the heathery sentimentality of Delius to hide that fact from himself.

By switching records on him, the girl forced him to face sensuality head-on. She wanted no pretense, but he couldn't do without it.

Emotional honesty about sex simply wasn't within his range. This habitual seducer had never really come to terms with the fairly obvious nature of his modus operandi. When forced to face his own lust unadorned—in fact, underscored by the rhythms of *Fire Dance*—he remained limp. So he and the girl just settled for a friendly beer.

The next day, desperate about his apparent impotence, this unusually naive young man came running for psychological counseling. A few casual interviews worked out to our mutual advantage. I owe him my acquaintance with Delius and de Falla, two composers previously unknown to me. In turn, I hope I helped him bridge more securely the categories of love and lust, which he had been able to reconcile only through music. This gain in sexual maturity might make him more selective and more constant in his affairs.

What relevance has this musical episode to obscenity? Simply this: the student used music in exactly the same way in which other men use four-letter words: to bridge in their own minds the cultural dichotomy between love and fuck. Just as the young man proved impotent without the proper kind of music to accomplish this purpose, many men depend on obscenity for adequate sexual performance.

Whether actually impotent or otherwise disturbed, many men cannot surmount the psychological hurdle posed by the cultural division between love and lust. A considerable proportion of personal and marital breakdowns are traceable to precisely this problem—the individual's inability to establish in his mind a workable connection between feeling and fucking.

The use of four-letter words in erotic situations is characteristic of such cases. Crude words are the battering ram with which the stymied male attempts to break down the artificial barrier between spirit and sensuality. With his four-letter blasts he is trying to clear the way toward the rather strenuous ideal of emancipated sex: the ultimate blending of love and fuck—spirit and body united: *e pluribus unum.*

Often a man's attempts to achieve fusion between love and fuck through the hot fury of dirty words defeat their own purpose. Instead of making love and lust coalesce into sexual harmony, obscenity sometimes separates the two elements still more widely.

The case of Robert and Dorothy Kramer exemplifies this syndrome. Many similar cases, being quite common, never receive any psychiatric attention at all. In their very ordinariness, they enter unremarked into the sum of psychocultural misery.

The Kramer's marriage had never been notably happy. A communicative block existed between the two partners from the beginning. But their sexual relations reached an intensity and degree of mutual satisfaction that at least partly made up for the shortcomings of their association.

Dorothy was severely masochistic and enjoyed verbal and physical humiliation. In fact, she could reach sexual responsiveness only after being throughly insulted.

Robert didn't have to be prodded. He bestowed verbal

abuse on his wife in generous measure, with a richly or-
chestrated vocabulary of sexual maledictions. This seemed
inconsistent with his usual mild manner but evidently
provided a compensatory mode of expression. He told me
that these four-letter tirades greatly increased both his
physical potency and his feeling of male dominance.

"It's power," he explained, "real power just to be cussing
her. And it registers on the meter." He smirked, casting his
eyes downward at his crotch.

His choice of words indicated that he regarded the
human body—and, by extension, the entire person—as a
purely mechanical device, a fairly typical attitude among
those whose mental-emotional life is conditioned by the
traditional body-spirit dualism of Christianity. This dualism often becomes intensified into a body *vs.* spirit antagonism which, supported by many factors in our culture,
often provides the starting split in a schizoid personality
structure.

In their own way, however, Robert and Dorothy seemed
suited to each other. As so often happens in a marriage
between masochistically and sadistically inclined persons,
each supplied the other's particular emotional and instinctual needs.

Yet few such strained harmonies can be lastingly sus-
tained. As long as a high degree of sexual attraction, based
largely on novelty, existed between Robert and Dorothy,
the marriage remained operational—to borrow a mecha-
nistic term Robert would have used. Yet as their sexual
excitability waned in time, the satisfying substance of their
relationship vanished. Only the ugly residue of obscene

language remained, serving more and more the purpose of expressing frustration, disappointment, and anger.

Increasingly, Robert berated his wife in the foulest of four-letter terms even in non-sexual everyday situations. With the tangible reality of sex gone, the verbal gestures were like shadowboxing—empty and unrewarding.

As long as dirty words culminated for Dorothy in a masochistic sex thrill, she couldn't get enough of them. But without the sexual sequel, her masochistic attitude vanished. No longer would she assume the role of the victim, listening contritely and helplessly to the abuse that represented a verbal surrogate of rape. She borrowed some of Robert's vocabulary and soon gave as good as she got. Symbolically, she usurped a masculine role. This in turn utterly undermined Robert's former notion of himself as the rough master of his household and left him totally unable to relate to his wife in any meaningful way. It was at this stage that Robert, then aged forty-five, came to consult me.

Analysis couldn't save Robert's marriage. There was, after all, nothing to save. The relationship had become useless. But the course of therapy revealed significant factors about Robert's need for obscenity in sexual situations.

Like many of middle-class background, he was deeply afraid of the aggressiveness inherent in male sexuality. He had been conditioned to believe that a wife was to be loved and cherished. Nothing had emotionally prepared him for the fact that, at times, she was also to be grabbed and screwed.

Fortunately this view of marital love as primarily spiritual is no longer strongly emphasized. This is not to say that spiritual love is unreal or absurd. When a man loves a landscape, a tree, a painting, a symphony, or an idea, that love can be overwhelmingly real and yet sexless. Absurdity arises from the treacly, traditional insistence that *all* great love must be—in the literal sense of the word—sublime. Love between men and women—within or without the connubial framework—just doesn't quite work that way. The failure of church and state (and their respective educational institutions) to face this fact has created phantom values that collapse under the touch of reality and often crush the individuals trying to uphold them. That is what had happened to Robert.

His upbringing never permitted him to realize that every sexual relationship contains an aggressive factor that exists alongside of its own sublimation. This aggressiveness is an important source of sexual vitality. As such it can function constructively within the total relationship.

Yet the aggressive factor can function constructively only if it is acknowledged and unrepressed. Men imbued with the fable that love is—or should be—all sweetness and light can find within this concept no useful employment for the aggressive side of their sexuality. Consequently, they repress it. In doing so, they block the possibility of sublimating their aggressions or displacing them into constructive forms.

In such cases, the repressed aggression often shows up in less acceptable guises. In extreme cases, murder and rape become the favored forms of sexual self-expression for such men. More often, obscenity provides a symbolic outlet for the repressed drives—which explains Robert's need for four-letter words as an aid to intercourse. Obscenity of this type performs a useful function: it releases repressed urges that might otherwise become extremely dangerous and destructive.

The connection between obscenity—particularly sexual obscenity—and violence is not always obvious. Robert, as I have already pointed out, is a deceptively mild-mannered person. By way of contrast, another patient of mine shows the link between obscenity and violence with rare directness.

Harold likes to pick fights. Nearly every week he is involved in some kind of serious melee, and he has served a number of jail sentences for assault. One phrase—"bloody fuck"—recurs in almost every one of his sentences, signifying his obsession with the idea of bloody violence. He knows that in England the word usually denotes merely mild annoyance or irritation. But Harold likes the word for its literal meaning and has been using it obsessively in that sense.

Sometimes he assaults people in the street, but he's no cowardly bully who picks on defenseless persons. He chooses rough and ready opponents and often takes them on two or three at a time in fantastic fistfights. Resulting injuries are sometimes serious enough to require hospitalization. From this he derives a tremendous feeling of power, tinged with sexual excitement.

On a typical occasion, Harold walked into a waterfront bar and ordered a Beefeater martini. When the drink was served, he shoved it aside without tasting it.

"You put in cheap gin," he accused the bartender.

The barkeep tried to cool down his scrappy customer with the kind of easygoing diplomacy that is part of his trade. But Harold wasn't having any of that. He escalated his insults until the bouncer eased him off the barstool.

That was the moment he had been waiting for. A short jab of his right put the bouncer off guard and a swing of the left laid him out. Immediately the bartender and a handful of steady customers joined forces against Harold.

Now he was in his element. With the battle cry of "bloody fuck" he lit into the huddle of adversaries and kept slugging until the cops pulled him loose. Only my testimony that he was under psychiatric care got him off with a suspended sentence.

He's been in other fights since. Jail doesn't scare him, nor does anything else. He goes on scrapping until he's either knocked out cold, hauled in by the police, or shipped to a hospital—or, as often happens, he manages to break loose and get away in search of the next adventure.

After each of these encounters, Harold feels extremely contrite. "I'm surprised I have survived this long," he once remarked to me wistfully. "Somebody may just knife me to death someday."

Harold himself never carries a weapon. He relies only on his fists. He takes great pride in the fact that every one of his knuckles has been broken by the power of his punch.

Once he was an alcoholic, but he had the strength of character to break the habit and stay on the wagon— evidence of a basically positive attitude toward life. Now he is trying to focus his great vitality in a struggle to free himself from his obsessive need for physical violence. At thirty-two, he's struggling for his future.

Obscenity plays an important part in this attempt. He deliberately tries to employ four-letter words as a surrogate for the physical act of aggression. But such stratagems, by their very nature, are apt to end in failure.

Recently, for example, he started swearing at some patrons in the West Side hash joint where he works as a short-order cook. For Harold, the swearing was a heroic effort to avoid direct violence. But for the patrons it was an obvious provocation. As might be expected, they failed to evaluate his insults in the light of his personal pathology. They took his curses at face value, and three of them ganged up on him. They were the worse for it in the end, and Harold was discouraged, too. Somehow he couldn't quite understand why those men didn't see that he swore at them only because he didn't really want to hit them. So *they* were the ones who forced him into a fight.

Harold's domestic life is similarly marked by a need for violence and an abundance of obscene language arising from this need. He lives with a handsome, tall girl in her middle twenties who's not afraid to hit back. Between them, they engage in incredible battles which usually end in passionate lovemaking. She doesn't really like these bouts, fearing that she might lose her teeth. Yet, without the violent prelude, sex relations between this couple simply don't take place.

It isn't that Harold—like some men—is impotent without the stimulus of violence. He has had intercourse without prior fights, but does not find it particularly rewarding. Without violence, there is for him less motivation toward sex.

In an effort to save their domestic situation, Harold and his girl, an intelligent young woman who holds a responsible job as a secretary, tried to substitute verbal for physical abuse. This proved quite satisfactory on several occasions, proving again that obscenity, as a form of verbal sadism, often serves as a surrogate for violence. At other times, however, the girl did not gauge her reactions carefully enough. She allowed her pride to get the better of her, and, when she did not accept insults meekly, the verbal exchange once again degenerated into slugging.

The girl, by the way, is by no means a hapless creature sacrificing herself to the unusual needs of her mate. She contributes her own share of incendiary hostility to the relationship. The first time she went to bed with Harold, he gave her gentlemanly warning of his violent propensities.

"Don't worry about me," she assured him. "I've slept with at least five hundred men."

Ever since, Harold feels himself surrounded by five hundred leering rivals every time he touches his girl.

"I'm not jealous," he insists. But he tells me that, every time he takes a swing at her, he symbolically knocks about at least one of the imaginary onlookers. But then there are still so many left.

And he keeps wondering why she kept count. "If a woman has eight or ten lovers," he says, "you'd expect her to keep score. But when you get above a hundred, what's the point? You couldn't tell them apart, anyhow.

"Avis," he quips, referring to the ads of the well-known car rental agency, "is only Number Two—and they're all steamed up about it. How do you think it feels to be Number 501?"

What bothers him is the anonymity of numbers. To be just another item on the assembly line, to have anonymity foisted on him in the most intimate of relations is unacceptable to his vital and self-assertive personality. He is determined to leave his distinctive mark. And he does it the only way he knows how—with his fists.

Harold's troubles began in childhood with brutal beatings administered to him regularly by his drunken father. Ever since he has been unable to separate love from violence, dependency from hate. This very ambivalence on Harold's part saved the father's life on one occasion when Harold resolved to murder him.

No sooner had Harold completed his rifle training in the army than he decided to apply his newly acquired skill to dispatch his father. He lurked in ambush, his rifle cocked and ready. But when his father ambled into sight, nothing happened.

"I was determined to do it," he told me. "I had the gun raised and I was tracking him. I held him in the gunsight as he walked. His ear was right on the crosshairs. I followed him with the gun until he had walked off. Only then I realized that I hadn't pulled the trigger."

This failure to carry out the planned killing further increased his need of violence. So great was this need that Harold almost constantly used foul language as a temporary substitute when no occasion for physical violence presented itself.

I have related Harold's behavioral syndrome in some detail because it reveals important factors often found in sexual obscenities. An insecure man may use obscenity prior to intercourse in order to reduce a woman to a status level at which he no longer needs to be afraid of her. (Harold, for example, was afraid of the father he both loved and hated. This constitutes a partial sexual block he could overcome only by a combination of obscenity and violence.)

Some men feel that, by degrading the woman symbolically through foul language, they may allow themselves greater sexual freedom than with the "undegraded" woman, whom they feel bound to respect. (Again, we note the separation of the love concept from the fuck concept.)

By his obscene language, Harold reduced the female—basically the mother—to a level of regression where she could be sexually overpowered without any awareness of incestual guilt. In this way he is also able at the same time to express sensual longing for the brutal, admired, yet feared rival-father. And by attacking males through obscene language and by random assault he indirectly punished the father for holding on to the sexually desired mother. The fight itself then assumes for Harold the role of a sadomasochistic love relationship.

Sometimes this need for preparatory obscenity in sexual encounters works the other way, the man requiring the woman to shower him with imprecations. Edmund Bergler, the great Viennese psychoanalyst, cites a classical case of this type—a man incapable of erection unless aroused by "filthy talk" from his partner. Virtually every prostitute has customers requiring verbal or physical abuse from her.

No matter whether the four-letter words are uttered by

the man or the woman, they serve notice on both partners that, at least for the time being, civilized rules of behavior are to be set aside in favor of what Wayland Young has termed "the jovial uproar of sensual fulfillment." Such a signal often helps normally inhibited persons to free themselves temporarily from the bonds of the superego and to break through the shame-barrier.

Yet obscenity is not a harmless aphrodisiac. The danger of destructive side effects always confronts those who rely on such basically unappetizing methods for sexual stimulation.

Sometimes, the train of arousal jumps the track. After the desired sexual release is obtained, normal inhibitions often cannot be restored at once. As a result, many couples find themselves engaged in vicious fights or verbal hostilities after intercourse.

A man using four-letter words to a woman symbolically asserts his power over her. In an important psychoanalytic paper on obscenity, Edmund Bergler tells of a patient who was in the habit of whispering obscene words of an anal character into the ears of strange women on the street. To his analyst, he expressed the following thought: "It is wonderful how with one word a man can embarrass a woman. First they blush with shame and then become furious. That they should blush and be discomfited is sufficient for me. It seems to me that I am a magician with unlimited power." Quite correctly, he understood his compulsion to be a form of sexual aggression and an assertion of dominance. This particular patient, a highly educated and witty man, once complained to his analyst about the injustice of the fact that poets, through the use of metaphor, were not only able to express the same suggestive ideas the patient wanted to whisper to women but even to acquire fame by doing so.

The question arises why a four-letter word whispered to a stranger should be so acutely embarrassing. The implied sexual proposition in itself, after all, need not be resented, though it may be ignored. In fact, women generally enjoy implied sexual propositions as long as nothing is said and done too explicity. That is the principle of flirtation. Why then has the four-letter word such a radically different effect?

One attempt at the answer can be found in a classic paper, one of the first systematic studies of obscenity, written in 1911 by Sandor Ferenczi. The author points out that, unlike most other words, the sexual four-letter word forces the person hearing it to visualize the anatomic parts or the physical action referred to. He speaks of the "visual imperative" exercised by obscene words. Because of the visual explicitness attached to four-letter language, obscene whispers addressed to a woman are psychologically equivalent to removing her clothes. Again there is the implied suggestion of violence and dominance.

As might be expected, most women experience revulsion at hearing four-letter words addressed to them. One of my patients, a woman brought up in a rigid, protected environment used to become frightened at even the most casual crudeness of speech heard in the company of men. Even such casual obscenities as "shit" or "crapped out" literally made her shiver. Through these words she was faced with thinking of human actions to which it was not permissible to allude in her home environment. This presented a problem because her boss, a TV network executive, whom she otherwise liked, was a rather rough-spoken man. Eventually she learned to assess and gauge the meaning of obscenity in different situations and to overcome her exaggerated fear of it.

A woman patient with whom I have explored this subject confided that she feels an acute sense of guilt whenever she hears obscenities. Just listening to such language, or witnessing an occasion where such language is used, makes her feel that she herself might be tempted to use four-letter words—an act incompatible with her self-image. She then feels that *she herself* is threatening the values which she had so far been able to maintain. Her ego defenses seem weakened, forcing her to regress to primitive, unacceptable levels of instinctual functioning, and thus causing considerable anxiety.

A woman's tendency or temptation to use four-letter words usually indicates subconscious rebellion against the female role and its socially imposed submissiveness, and thus transition to more aggressive or exhibitionistic modes of conduct. I have observed that women who have either left their husbands or have been deserted by them tend to adopt obscenity patterns in their speech when they assume the traditionally male responsibilities of supporting and guiding the family. This seems to be as true for the fashionable and fancy-hatted woman executive on Madison Avenue as for the resolute Harlem mother trying to manage her family in the absence of a male. In either case, the four-letter word becomes the badge of social dominance. The woman serves symbolic notice that she has, along with the male's economic role, assumed his authority status.

The exact manifestations of this process vary with the milieu. A lady editor may allow herself an exasperated "shoot" over a misplaced comma while the carhop at some drive-in may enjoin a pestering fellow worker to "fuck off." In family situations where the male has abdicated his traditional role as a provider but remains on the scene as a freeloader, the woman often adopts obscene language to signify that she—the big She with the capital S —has taken over the male prerogatives and has assumed the power of a matriarch. In this reversal of roles, the four-letter word becomes the blunt stamp that marks the useless male as a drone.

Only one kind of woman seems to enjoy having obscenity directed at her—the severely masochistic type. Such women have told me that obscenity, rather than causing them fright or revulsion, seems to stimulate them sexually. Men are usally quick to recognize and capitalize on this response. As a result, such women are particularly prone to seduction by the cruder kind of males.

Much of this chapter has dealt with clinical situations. The advantage of citing such situations is that they represent salient factors in a fully developed and more clearly apparent form. Yet in conclusion, it should again be emphasized that a basic four-letter attitude toward sex is by no means confined to persons so severely disturbed as to require psychiatric aid. On the contrary, the four-letter attitude—springing from the ambivalence between the concepts of love and fuck—is endemic in our culture.

This ambivalence, expressed by Clifford Odets in our opening quotation of "Listen, lousy . . . ," runs as a constant theme through modern American literature. Nearly every modern popular novel, whether written by a perceptive man like Norman Mailer or by some formula hack, portrays at least one figure as rigidly stereotyped as the characters of the comedia dell'arte. He is the potent male in search of sexual fulfillment who cannot satisfy his longings in normal love relationships. He craves a sort of illegitimate excitement at some impossible locus of the sexual fantasy that combines the exciting freshness of smart seduction or casual rape with the comforts of a penthouse harem.

Here the paradox grows. As the American hero sets out to seek the Holy Grail of sex—the summum bonum of our century—he learns en route that sex is exciting to him only if it is somehow dirty. It is at this point that his need to idealize and his need to degrade merge. The novelist is thus led to produce a miasmal hash of intellectually stillborn and sentimentally swaddled rationalizations. The language nearly always includes a generous sprinkling of obscene references, and the ultimate philosophy can be summed up as the elevation of adolescent fantasy to the level of esthetic theory.

The bridge between literature and life is surprisingly direct. Men have come to my office complaining of pathetic feelings of personal insufficiency simply because in real life they can't quite make the grade in literary terms.

They are in deep spiritual doubt because they can't live up to the Gospel according to *Playboy* or *Evergreen Review*.

Some altogether competent young men—and lately even some young women—worry about being too "hung up" on the more earnest aspects of love and personal devotion. They think they're missing out on the more carefree aspects of sensuality that they consider their birthright, and they may even feel seriously remiss in what they believe to be their moral obligation to enjoy life to the fullest. In short, modern literature has made "fucking around" a new orthodoxy to which some young people religiously adhere.

Conversely, I have encountered inveterate young swingers who aren't carefree at all but worry that their touch-and-go kind of sex makes them miss the rewards of more lasting emotional commitments. The tensions generated by such conflicts are often expressed in colorful four-letter terms.

Unless such problems are accompanied by more substantial personality disorders, I do not regard them as anything more serious than the growing pains of a culture that after some five thousand years of institutionalized sexual repression has finally reached a stage of awareness. With luck and a modicum of intelligence we may outgrow this ambivalence of our sexual values in about one more generation.

5. Dirty Magic

Some years ago, wandering among the guests at a Bar Mitzvah, I was introduced to Dr. John Adams, who, as an anthropologist, had a more or less professional interest in the event. After the initial formalities, our talk turned, naturally enough, to initiation rites.

Dr. Adams deplored the fact that, in our present setting, a Bar Mitzvah is no longer operational: thirteen-year-old boys in modern America aren't really entering manhood.

"We no longer have a clear demarcation line between child and adult," Dr. Adams observed. "That's what's causing all the troubles of adolescence."

Evidently we had hit on an area where both our professional interests joined. So, after one more raid on the buffet, we made for a relatively quiet corner. Dr. Adams, who at that time was on the faculty of George Washington University in St. Louis, propounded his belief that the prevalent identity crises among young Americans may be caused by the lack of effective initiation rites in our culture.

"You've got to separate the men from the boys in a

really dramatic way that leaves no doubt about who's what," he observed. "All this is very pleasant," he said, gesturing toward the canapé-munching and sherry-sipping assemblage. "But it doesn't make the point strongly enough. Truly effective ritual must be dramatic. It must employ shock tactics to permanently mark the awareness of everyone involved. Take an African 'Bar Mitzvah,' for example."

He outlined the rites of the Akambas of Tanganyika, where pubertal boys are taken into the jungle by the older men of the tribe for a two-week-long romp. At the crucial moment of the ceremony, the older men induce an erection among the boys, who thereupon dig their erect penises into the soft ground, signifying union with Mother Earth. During this orgiastic plowing and seeding, both the boys and the older men chant obscenities.

Normally, Dr. Adams explained, the Akambas wouldn't consider this behavior proper. But ritual taboo-breaking and foul-mouthed harangues are frequently part of religious ceremony among primitives. He had, by the way, a workable definition for primitives: "people who have been spared contact with Europeans."

It was this informal encounter that prompted me to reflect at some length on the intricate and often paradoxical relations between the obscene, the forbidden, and sacred.

The concepts of obscenity and taboo necessarily overlap. Obscenity is that which we are not allowed to say. Taboo is that which we are not allowed to do. By extension, a taboo act is in itself an obscenity. To the extent of their overlap, the two terms may therefore be used interchangeably.

In modern western society, the forbidden is often sexual in nature. Other societies sometimes have other taboos, hence other obscenities.

Inviting a young lady for dinner is quite acceptable hereabouts. But don't try it if she's a Trobriander. For these people, public eating is obscene. Food must be taken in privacy—and it is especially important that no person of the opposite sex sees you eat. The Fiji feel the same way about meals, and they are very neat about cleaning up. They never leave any trace of food. The obscenities of these tribes presumably have to do with their table manners.

Inviting a young lady to bed, on the other hand, is a rather tricky undertaking in western society. At least in polite circles, it involves a great deal of ritual coaxing. A Trobriander, by contrast, would hardly comprehend our elaborate ceremonies of courtship or seduction. On his island, men and women are cheerfully uninhibited and frankly sensual. Sexual prowess, measured by skill rather than frequency, is a mark of good citizenship in his community.

In matters of sexual freedom, the Australian aborigines are the unquestioned champions. In his excellent study of puberty rites, *Symbolic Wounds,* Bruno Bettelheim lyrically sums up the sexual scene down under:

". . . children are allowed to indulge sexual desires without criticism. They may be invited by a mother, older brother or sister, or some other person to have sexual intercourse with an adult or a child of the same age standing nearby. Their sexual organs may be played with or their sexual potentialities discussed at length and in detail in the hearing of older persons. At an early age they learn of the sexual act by direct observation, and they imitate sexual activities among themselves, publicly when they are very young and somewhat more privately when they become older and more self-conscious. With increasing age the child's sexual behavior, though remaining free, comes to resemble adult sexual activity more closely."

Bettelheim contrasts this with the upbringing of American children, who are "presented with a very limited number of libidinal choices," and among whom the mother plays a special role. Still speaking of the Australians, Bettelheim observes further, "The emotional closeness of the modern Western family, with its restrictions concerning cleanliness, movement, noise, and touch—all of which set the stage for castration anxiety—is absent."

Since obscenity as we know it grows largely from precisely such restrictions and anxieties, I have often wondered what forms obscenity takes in these ultra-permissive Australian cultures. Unfortunately, no such data appear to be available, a fact that might well be noted by a travel-hungry graduate student in search of a thesis subject.

As an invocation of magic powers, obscenity belongs to the same class of utterance as the curse or the prayer. This may be why in primitive societies so close a link remains between obscenity and ritual observance, centering on the mystery of the forbidden.

The forbidden, as a rule, is dirty and holy at the same time. In Christian cultures the emotional ambivalence about love and sex reflects this. To the theologically oriented Christian, love and sex are the two opposite poles of a holy-dirty continuum, and he's got to pick his own place somewhere along the line. It is significant that, in this same theology, Lucifer, the embodiment of evil, is really a fallen angel. In short, that which is obscene and unspeakable is at the same time that which—until relegated to hell—was sacred *beyond* language.

At bottom, the mysteries of sex, or plant growth (even when tamed in agriculture), or of familial love and loyalty are indeed beyond language. Here then lies the raw material from which obscenity is fashioned.

Obscenity grows from that which is holy and mysterious by an odd switch—throwing the original values in reverse.

A case in point is that of the pig. Throughout the early cultures of the Near East, the pig was a sacred animal. As such, it was not eaten. Later on, when the Semites established domination of the area, they fashioned new myths and orthodoxies to bolster their territorial and political control. One of the basic techniques in the manufacture of new orthodoxies is to reverse earlier myths—as any propagandist knows. In this process of value reversal, the sacred pig became the dirty, unkosher pig.

The fact that sacred animals were never eaten was useful to the Semites. For it would have been more difficult to challenge the culinary attractions of pork than to change the image of the pig. The earliest rabbinical reasoning on this subject (if one may reconstruct it in capsule form) might have been: the beast is uneatable, anyway, and we need some new interpretation of the old taboo. From here on, let's say the pig is dirty instead of holy.

Later of course, the subject was expanded into many elegantly constructed Hebrew treatises that are now part of the sacred writings of Judaism. Their arguments must be persuasive indeed, because, in point of pigs, even the Arabs side with the Jews.

At the time of the Crusades, anti-pig sentiment spread from the Arab world into medievally crude Europe, jointly with such other Arab specialties as astronomy, mathematics, physics, and the notion of romantic love. All of these were enthusiastically taken up by Europeans; and today, along with science and sentimental love, a great variety of pig-centered obscenities exists in the national cultures of Europe.

German, for instance, has countless categories of obscene appellations based on *"Schwein."* The structure of the language, permitting the construction of long, compound nouns, makes it possible for Germans to incorporate piggishness—at least linguistically—into practically everything.

The Italians, lacking the device of the compound noun, are confined to the use of *"porco!"* as a simple expletive; but the word makes up in emotional weight what it lacks in semantic elaboration.

One could trace obscene connotations of the word for "pig" in practically all European languages, with every shade of snickering reprobation woven around *"cochon," "puerco," "gris," "svin,"* and others. Only English should be exempted from the list. For, unlike its counterpart in most other European languages, the English word "pig" as applied to a person often means that he is merely physically rather than morally dirty.

Only in one form does the pre-Semitic character of the pig as protective idol survive in our culture. As a repository for coins, its sacred character remains unquestioned.

While the social history of the pig (as seen from the human point of view) shows a value transformation from sacred to obscene, such transformations also occur in the other direction. As we have already mentioned, under certain conditions the practice of what is normally regarded as obscene becomes a sacred act.

Sexual intercourse between parents and children, for example, is so strongly taboo in most societies that the mere mention of it constitutes an obscenity. Yet the Swiss anthropologist Henri Junod reports in his epochal study, *The Life of a South African Tribe*, that in times of crisis the magic power of the taboo is invoked by ceremonially violating it. During prolonged spells of bad weather or in wartime, the tribal fathers—in obvious terror at their own doing—fall upon their sons and daughters, hoping that the mysterious powers behind the taboo will thereby be alerted to the tribe's troubles. Incest thus becomes a patriotic duty.

This value reversal of turning a normally criminal and obscene act into a holy exercise should not surprise westerners, who undergo the same process. Murder, for example, is normally considered reprehensible in Judeo-Christian civilizations. Strong taboos are spelled out against it in both clerical and secular law. Yet in tribal (or national) crises, such as war, the same value reversal takes place as in the previously mentioned African tribes. We are thus treated to the curious spectacle of priests, ministers, and rabbis holding forth on the nobility of military valor and trying to enlist the same God on both sides. Again, the taboo is deliberately violated, and what is normally regarded as debased is elevated as virtue.

In studying the obscenities of exotic cultures, the western observer is always handicapped. For one thing, there's the language barrier. A diligent anthropologist may become reasonably fluent in some Bantu or Zulu dialect; yet even so he is likely to have difficulty in telling a proper word from an improper one. And even if he wins the friendship and confidence of the people he is studying, they are apt to be on their good behavior in his presence, since he is a visitor. His opportunities to observe the coarser aspects of native obscenity are therefore limited.

In view of these handicaps it is surprising how much of the nature of primitive taboo and obscenity has been learned by western observers. Among the vast variety of material available, I should merely like to point to a few cases that seem particularly relevant—either by contrast or parallel—to the types of obscenity encountered in our own culture.

One of the oddest forms of obscenity is found among the Eskimo. In his monumental three-volume work, *The Intellectual Life of the Eskimo,* Knud Rasmussen reports that a man's name becomes taboo for a period of up to three years following his death. Unfortunately, Eskimo men have compound names made up of common and highly utilitarian words. A man, for example, might be named "He-Who-Steers-Swiftly-the-Safe-Canoe." Imagine the linguistic calamity when he dies. The words "steer," "swift," "safe," and "canoe" become ipso facto obscene, leaving an awkward lack in the language.

The perennial word shortage caused by human mortality made it necessary to invent new words as more people died. In this way, the language, initially poor in synonyms, gradually developed enough alternate words so that nowadays the Eskimos aren't literally left speechless by the normal death rate.

The Zulu in Africa have similar problems, because no one may utter the names of the progenitors of the tribal chief for as many generations back as anyone remembers. Here too, the names are common nouns; and matters are made worse because similar-sounding or rhyming words are also considered obscene.

What is probably the most elaborate linguistic taboo is found in Laos, where nearly all common words become obscene to a man while engaged in hunting elephants. He is obliged to provide himself with a special language for such occasions.

Similarly, many European languages develop spare words to take the place of those which have become tinged with obscenity. In English, for example, old Saxon words describing the bodily functions remain in use but are considered vulgar, if not outright obscene, while later imports of Latin derivation have taken over as respectable substitutes. When we "eliminate" instead of "shit," or "copulate" instead of "fuck," we participate in a linguistic ritual similar to that of the Eskimo or the Laotian elephant hunter.

In a reductio ad absurdum of this process, even an outspoken writer like Richard von Krafft-Ebing switches to Latin entirely whenever he has something overly anatomic to describe.

The search for "respectable" synonyms is by no means confined to matters of our own anatomy. The linguistic effort to clothe the naked flesh with the opacity of a foreign language extends even to the beasts.

The names of domestic animals in English have remained Saxon, while their meat, as if to make it more fit to appear on the dining table, has been given Norman names. So we have cattle transformed into beef, calf into veal, sheep into mutton, and deer into venison. To say one had bullmeat, oxmeat, or cowmeat for supper, aside from being eccentric, would surely sound unseemly.

In the fifteenth century, the Scottish poet William Dunbar was so enraged by this process, which he considered an unwarranted dilution of language, that he composed a nameless poem which a later editor, William McKay MacKenzie, entitled *Overheard in the Hedgerow*. The poet pictures himself eavesdropping on two lovers in the bushes who have apparently heard neither of Norman words nor of French notions of courtly love. The poem then evolves into a lexicon of love in the simplest Saxon terms. It was Dunbar's futile protest against the course of linguistic history which had transformed the treasured, traditional words of endearment and lovemaking of the Scottish people into latter-day obscenities.

It seems odd, that, while popular sexual terms change frequently, simple curses are remarkably constant. A modern reader looking at Middle-English prose or poetry will find fairly few words immediately recognizable, but the cuss words will leap from the page to greet him as old—old indeed—acquaintances.

Word magic of the most primitive type still survives in the northern British Isles, where, even today, fishermen will return to harbor if anyone in the boat mentions the words "pig," "sow," or "swine." Only if an iron nail is touched while calling out "cauld airn" is the pig-spell vitiated. W. Gregor reports in *The Folklore of the Northeast and Scotland* that a good many Scots think it is wise to touch the nails of their shoes in church and mutter "cauld airn" if the clergyman reads the parable of the Gadarene swine.

Ceremonial obscenity, in word and deed, has been amply documented in Sir James George Frazer's classic compendium, *The Golden Bough*. He tells us, for example, that the Kaffirs believe in climate control by means of dirty words. Dry spells are ended by a little girl filling a calabash with beetles. The girl then throws the calabash with its insect inmates into a lake. As the crawly missile splashes down, a waiting chorus of women bursts out into obscene yells which, as Sir James primly notes, "they would never dare utter except on this occasion."

Other tribes (for example the Ba-Thonga Bantus of South Africa) are quite sure what causes the dry spells in the first place, and have a remedy to match. A woman's miscarriage stops the rain. To end the drought, they dig up the remains of the abortion and ask some ritual questions of a bystanding group of men, whose answer is a filthy harangue.

The harvest festivals of pre-Homeric Greece, like modern sales meetings, began with formal swapping of dirty jokes; and the hors d'oeuvres, according to Frazer, consisted of little pastries "baked in the form of male and female organs of generation." From that point on, talk, songs, and action grew progressively less inhibited, and, as some pre-Homeric scribe may have reported, "a good time was had by all."

This was too much for Sir James. That sort of thing was all right, perhaps, for Zulus, Bantus, and such. But Sir James, brought up to revere the classics, simply could not bring himself to view the ancient Greeks as dispassionately as he would have looked at contemporary Africans. So he adds the following bit of anthropologic whitewash to his description of the Greek festivities: "If these particulars are correctly reported, we may suppose that these indecencies, like certain obscenities which seem to have formed part of the Great Mysteries at Eleusis, were no mere wanton outbursts of licentious passion, but were deliberately practiced rites calculated to promote the fertility of the ground by means of homeopathic or imitative magic."

Unwittingly, Sir James has given us more anthropological data than he intended: a portrait of the author as Victorian Englishman. He could not deny what the Greeks did. But at least he could suggest that they didn't do it for fun. It was simply their agricultural duty, he implied.

Other opportunities for speculating about the mingling of the holy and the obscene have been provided by various forms of sacred prostitution. While in western society prostitution is nowadays considered a shameful practice, one form of it is still regarded as sacred in India. The word for the holy prostitutes of Madras translates literally as "handmaidens of the gods." Even their pimps are persons held in esteem and veneration, having assumed the status of Hindu priests.

A different yet related way of combining sex and mysticism is the orgy. Communal sex may fail to entice persons imbued with a monogamistic outlook, but, in its ability to transform the individual personality, the orgy is undoubtedly a highly effective form of "magic." It is significant that cults practicing sex en masse are now springing up in the larger cities of the United States and western Europe. I am not referring to the frivolous "swingers"— wife-swapping clubs with assignations arranged, among other ways, by mail. Rather, I have in mind certain neo-mystic groups of serious people in which each member is encouraged (though not required) to have sex relations with as many other members of the group as he or she can manage. This exercise is prompted neither by hedonism nor licentiousness. Rather, it is felt that sexual round robins help obliterate the sense of personal separateness which mystics regard as a barrier to revelation.

Pooled sex, according to these neo-mystic theories, leads to spiritual as well as physical merging, thus enabling each participant to partake in a "greater" selfhood, not confined to the limits of his own individuality. As modern counterparts of ancient orgiastic rites, these practices attempt to restore a sense of communal sharing and belonging largely lost in today's world.

From a psychological point of view, this seems like just so much rationalization, disguising the fact that orgiastic sex is by definition depersonalized and antithetical to any possibility of sharing beyond the physiologic level. The emotional basis of an orgy is more masturbatory than mystical, more narcissistic than outgoing.

Just as the orgiastic element tends to depersonalize sex itself, the absence of restraint also tends to dilute the emotional charge of four-letter words.

With the progressive relaxation of sexual mores, the pejorative weight of these words has been lessened, their "dirty magic" dissipated. The British writer Geoffrey Gorer suggests in his now-classic essay *The Pornography of Death* that our primary taboo has shifted in the twentieth century. He argues that sex is no longer really objectionable; a new "unmentionable" has arisen: death.

In an era of unprecedented slaughter by war, political terrorism, and automobile, Gorer believes that sudden and violent death has become intensified as a focus of fear, while sex has lost both its horror and attraction. As a result, many people feel the same squeamishness in talking of death that Victorians used to feel in talking of sex.

"Our grandparents were told that babies were found under gooseberry bushes or cabbages," writes Gorer. "Our children are more likely to be told that those who have passed on (fie! on the gross Anglo-Saxon monosyllable) are changed into flowers or rest in lovely gardens. . . . The art of the embalmers is an art of complete denial." Where once the facts of sex were hidden, he notes, we now hide the facts of death.

Language lags behind culture, and it may be some time until this value shift is clearly reflected in our vocabulary. Yet eventually the sexual vernacular may entirely lose both the stigma and force of obscenity while a new dirty vulgate sprouts around that inexorably final four-letter word, "dead."

No matter what specific form it may take, obscenity serves as a talisman—a dirty magic by which we attempt to control the environment. The mechanism is somewhat indirect and underhanded. In uttering the obscenity we violate the taboo; and in violating the taboo we stir the mysterious powers behind the forbidden. It's getting at the gods through the back door.

Emotionally, this adds up to a double payoff. We gain our symbolic security by setting up the ritual and observing its taboos. Then we cash in an extra emotional dividend by knocking down the whole symbolic structure with an obscenity. In short, ritual observance of taboo has both a positive and negative phase. Obscenity is the negative phase.

Basic taboos, designed to instill feelings of security, are often sensual prohibitions: don't touch, don't look, don't eat, and so on. Usually they involve self-denial; for, as Freud observed, "Things that are not desired are not forbidden." We curry the favor of the magic powers— divine or otherwise—by observing these restrictions. By performing the rituals and abstaining from the taboos we gain the illusion of being in control of the world, or at least on the good side of its ruling forces. Up to a point, anyway.

When that point is passed, the negative phase begins. Under pressure of crisis, we lose confidence in the normal ritual. The very fact that the crisis exists proves to us that the normal ritual isn't getting us all the magic help we need. So, to squeeze out some extra magic from the taboo, we put it in reverse. This is the time when African fathers rape their children and the good suburban housewife goes upstairs with the milkman. From these acts they gain re-assurance—at least for the moment—no matter what the ultimate consequence.

Since few of us are ever desperate enough to commit such cataclysmic acts to relieve our anxieties, a less drastic substitute is needed. Verbal obscenity provides this sur-rogate, substituting word for action. Yet, often, respect-able members of the tribe can't even afford an obscene outburst without losing status. Hence they require the services of a shaman, a "sinful" priest or medicine man whose deliberate obscenities or outrages represent their own rebellion. The shaman violates our taboos for us. He gives us the emotional bonus gained from the negative phase of ritual—without our getting ourselves dirty.

In western cultures, the role of the shaman has often been assumed by alienated entertainers,—the court fool of the middle ages, and today's "black humorist."

Alienation bestows privilege on such men. Standing out-side the social norm, they constitute no direct threat to the established power structure. Consequently, they get away with saying and doing things that would be un-thinkable for others. But in uttering obscenities and in chal-lenging orthodoxies, they keep the community from being suffocated by the stuffiness of its solid citizens. Their special freedom permits them to present stale and some-times pernicious orthodoxies in a new and liberating perspective. As licensed critics, they cut holes into the social fabric to let some fresh air in.

In October 1963 *Commentary* carried a remarkable essay by Albert Goldman, likening the then living comedian Lenny Bruce to a shaman for the American middle class. Bruce's notorious use of obscenity and his relentless attacks on fashionable sacred cows, Goldman suggests, administered a brutal but needed cathartic to the fatuous conformities of the American establishment.

"Bruce has indeed become the shaman," writes Goldman. "He has taken on himself the role of exorcising the private fears and submerged fantasies of the public by articulating in comic form the rage and nihilistic savagery hidden beneath the lid of social inhibition."

Lately the role of the modern shaman appears to be taken up not only by singular entertainers but by groups as well. A remarkably unfettered case in point is an anarchic gang of performers operating under the blandly evocative name of "The Fugs." "They are neither art nor theater," observes one critic. "Still, they make all sorts of popular entertainment obsolete."

What is superseded in the The Fugs' frequently obscene assault on society is the tradition of sentimentality that has dominated the commercial theater since its inception, and, through the mediums of films and TV, still sets spurious social standards. "Sentimentality," notes *The New York Review*, "is often the handmaiden of moral and political instruction. This is the most melancholy union of all."

It is against this "melancholy union" that The Fugs aim

their iconoclasm. Instead of offering lessons in orthodox unreality in the manner of conventional entertainments, The Fugs invite their audience to "group grope" for more viable values. Notes *The New York Review*, "The Fugs are idealogues of some kind, not orgiasts."

The first job of the ideologic comedian is to clear out culturally accreted rubbish. In this herculean task, the dirty word is his cleaning tool.

The Fugs' frontal assault on stale, stylized sentiment is staged to the tune of a song titled "My Baby Done Left Me and I feel like Homemade Shit." The strategy is clear. In combining the word "homemade" with "shit," they are heightening an obscenity that has already passed so completely into the general vocabulary that it has lost its basic emotional power. But they have recharged the excremental word by relating it to mother and apple pie. The revitalized obscenity now has the energy to assault the holiest of middle-class bastions. This is the work of a modern shaman.

Today's shaman is a symbol-slinger. In other words, he has to be poetic. He can no longer use unvarnished obscenity because it no longer penetrates. The need for poetically obscene symbol manipulation may be the key to the success of such writer-reciters as Allen Ginsberg and to the increasing influence of a new theatrical art form: the cabaret of exorcism. To shout the unspeakable becomes part of a cultural purification rite.

Thus the outer-fringe cabaret becomes the true mystery play of our century, the place where tradition is scrubbed with a scouring obscenity until it is reshaped into new values. And so our own obscenity rites are linked with the primitive practices described earlier. The dirty magic is still potent, reminding us that all humanity grows on the same golden bough.

6. When Children Play the Game

Andy, age six, had just been let off by the school bus at the rose-entwined gate of his home in neatest Connecticut. To his mother, rushing out to greet him, he said curtly: "Shit!" Then he stood quietly, watching.

Andy's mother, an even-tempered and permissive paragon of modernity in child-rearing, managed to seem unimpressed.

So Andy had to try his gambit again. His mother suggested that it would be better to say he was going to have a "B.M." But evidently that wasn't at all what Andy had in mind.

Soon Andy's use of the word "shit" assumed a nearly obsessive frequency, and I was asked to find out what was wrong with the boy. I reassured Andy's mother that her little boy's case was by no means unusual. Many children discover during their early school years that dirty words are remarkably effective devices for controlling their parents. Andy knew his mother well enough not to be fooled by her pretended nonchalance. He sensed quite accurately that "shit" shocked her, and he was going to make the most of it.

Episodes like these are typical among middle-class children brought up in the isolated protection of suburban environments. Their entry into school usually marks their first chance to enlarge their vocabularies with terms not encountered in their families or immediate peer groups. Nobody has to tell the children that these words are "dirty." Their taboo character is evident from the clandestine manner in which they are shared. Moreover, the almost ritual utterance of these words is surrounded by a palpable aura of tense eroticism, often tinged with sadistic overtones.

The middle-class child, characteristically fenced in by parental regard for proprieties and conventions, jubilantly embraces the dirty word as a handy fence-buster. The obscene word becomes his libertarian slogan against the restrictive force of established order. He raises it as a battle cry against the enemy land of collective adulthood. For him, there is an explorer's joy in the fresh discovery of dirty words, an elation denied the lower-class child, in whose world dirty talk is common.

Seizing this exciting new vocabulary as an instrument of domination, the middle-class child finds at his disposal a weapon of sufficient shock power to dent the defenses of the adult world, which on most other occasions have proved so infuriatingly impervious to childish onslaught.

That Andy has chosen to employ "shit" as his principal weapon has an added significance. His off-color vocabulary, as our later talks confirmed, was considerably more extensive. But "shit" had a special meaning. It was a symbolic protest against parental discipline, filed by way of the anus—the child's main channel for registering dissent.

Even before protest takes verbal form, the anus becomes the child's center of anti-authoritarian expression when, in spite or rage, he reneges on his toilet training. Only with great reluctance does the growing child relinquish such revolutionary gestures in later years, when defecating in his pants becomes incompatible with the young rebel's dignity.

With his principal protest device thus made obsolete, he casts about for some alternate weapon with which to arm himself for the relentless battle with his parents. It is at this stage that he discovers the psychological warfare potential of four-letter words.

Where in younger years he might have smeared himself all over with his feces to express his disdain for parentally imposed taboos, or might have consistently wet his bed to manifest his unwillingness to grow up, he now confronts his parents with his newly acquired scatological vocabulary, thus serving notice that he means to hold onto the proven techniques of anal aggression—at least on the symbolic level.

When anal conditioning of behavior was discussed some years ago at a seminar broadly encompassing many areas of behavioral science, an astute young historian pointed out that such anal factors are evident in the usual adult reaction to cultural change. Here, too, the anally oriented person insists on simpler, if outmoded, methods in his encounters with complex and changing realities. Resistance to change in any form is characteristic of anal-retentive personalities. As an example, the young historian cited our military establishment which—in the nuclear age—still rattles verbal sabers to achieve purposes which in themselves are no longer realistic. Quite aptly, he linked this historic sidelight to a child's futile reliance on anal action or vocabulary to deal with realities in later life that are in fact too complex to be controlled with his sphincter.

Such anal modes of action or expression usually stem from neurotic fear of facing new situations creatively. While much of human behavior, both in children and in adults, is determined in this way, the anal origin of such behavior, unfortunately, is often camouflaged. Rarely is it as evident as in the "Bronx cheer," that marvelously direct, bottom-glorifying and thought-shunting all-purpose negative comment.

Like the Bronx cheer, the child's utterance of a scatologic word serves as an oral equivalent of flatus. Instead of expelling the "dirty" gas through his rear, he spews forth a dirty word from his mouth.

It is not poetic metaphor to describe such utterance as an oral fart. That term precisely and realistically describes the bodily condition that, in various degrees, accompanies a child's obscenity. Children severely resentful of parental discipline or authority sometimes exhibit reverse peristalsis. The movement of their intestines and gullet runs backward, causing severe vomiting and, after they run out of disposable matter from their stomachs, the expulsion of feces from the mouth. If resentful utterance does not reach the point of oral defecation but remains confined to scatologic words, these words function as substitutes for the fecal matter.

The phenomenon, either in its fecal or verbal form, is nearly always traceable to some anti-authoritarian reaction. My first step in the treatment of such cases, therefore, is to caution parents against regarding such children as willfully naughty. I point out that sharpened discipline will only aggravate a situation caused by parental over-control in the first place. Often the child has little or no power over symptoms stemming from resentments he may not consciously realize.

On the conscious level, the child may wish to conform to the parental demand for fecal cleanliness and sphincter control, but, if this demand is presented too early in life and in unacceptably authoritarian terms, the child may *unintentionally* resort to such devious tokens of rebellion as a symbolic loss of bowel control by the expelling of dirty words from his mouth. The age group of from four to six years is particularly susceptible to disturbances of this type, though the syndrome sometimes appears as late as the age of eight.

Timing of toilet training, many parents believe, is of paramount importance in avoiding such difficulties. My own observation is that timing is far less significant than parental attitude. Granted, too early attempts at toilet training predispose the child toward disturbances of this type, as would undue delay of training. The really harmful factor, however, is ferocious and punitive insistence on rectal continence.

By no means are all children who display excessive fondness for scatologic words to be considered deeply traumatized. Moderate use of scatologic terms by youngsters in this age group is in most cases a normal part of their struggle for pseudo-adult supremacy. Because the child wishes to usurp the adult role, he takes delight in shocking the adult by any possible means. A slingshot is the traditional instrument employed for this purpose. But the child discovers that slinging verbal dirt is just as effective.

The permissively raised Andy proved a case in point. No deep-seated resentments distorted the mind of this cheerful child. A few casual questions revealed what was bothering him. His mother was always "going out" or "getting ready." She was involved in dozens of groups in her community, and there was little time for Andy. For him, the miracle of "shit" was that it stopped Mother in her ever-busy tracks. True, she was playing it cool, and Andy admitted that the word had less effect than he had hoped. But for a moment, anyway, it made her turn around and look at Andy. As so often in cases involving a child's use of obscenity, the problem was really the parent's, not the child's.

A more complex causation, involving considerable psychic trauma, was evident in the case of a girl I treated recently for a condition which included, among other symptoms, the compulsive use of obscenity. The case illustrated many of the psychodynamic forces commonly encountered in such situations.

Gail's mother, a lower-class woman with rather rigid attitudes, brought her daughter to me because the girl had suddenly begun to stammer at the age of eight. This in itself was unusual, for the onset of stammering generally occurs at a far earlier age. The first few interviews disclosed that Gail had undergone a prolonged and traumatic period of toilet training. Even at the age of six, she had not yet learned to control her rectum, and both parents beat her whenever she had an unexpected bowel movement. It is hardly surprising that these draconic measures resulted in intense hostility of the girl toward her parents, which Gail freely and venomously expressed to me as soon as her mother left the consulting room. Significantly, the girl did not stammer during these outbursts.

I had long been inured to the fact that most women and children are in full command of a vocabulary commonly presumed to be known only to sailors, but the meaty orchestration of little Gail's maledictions prompted me to ask where she had learned those words.

"From the other girls at our playground," she said without a trace of self-consciousness.

Gail lost no time in making good use of her language lessons. No sooner had she acquired a new obscenity than she immediately loosed it on her parents as a token of hostility and aggression. The parents' response was exactly the same as toward her defective toilet training: they beat her some more.

At this point, the girl began to stammer. Psychologically, this reaction was quite natural—almost predictable. Obscenity was the most useful and the most deeply treasured aspect of this child's language. It was her way of verbally defecating on her parents, just as she symbolically defecated on them by the incontinence of her bowels. When parental beatings deprived her of the part of her vocabulary that was emotionally the most essential to her, she symbolically renounced language altogether by developing her speech defect.

Gail's general prognosis was rather poor, partly because of certain pre-schizophrenic tendencies, partly because her parents' rigidity of attitude made it difficult to establish the kind of rapport between them and the girl that might eventually have dispelled the predominant atmosphere of antagonism. Yet despite these handicaps, Gail's stammer disappeared after a series of psychiatric interviews.

By far the oddest case of compulsive juvenile obscenity I ever encountered was that of a fifteen-year-old boy of middle-class Jewish background whose singular fascination was meteorology. He had acquired considerable knowledge of the field, read voraciously in it, talked of nothing else, forecast the weather with astonishing accuracy, and—despite his high intelligence—failed all his subjects in school.

Bernie's teachers complained that he paid no attention in class—at least not to them. Instead, he concentrated on the meteorology books he constantly studied and restudied under his desk. At home, his behavior was similar. He ignored his family and locked himself in his room with his books. His obsession with this particular branch of science led to an almost total withdrawal.

Bernie's isolation was largely the fault of his family. Not only did they fail to share, let alone encourage, his remarkable interest; they actively ridiculed it. Despite the fact that his weather predictions, by taking careful account of local conditions, often proved more specific and reliable than official forecasts for the area, nobody took his devoted work and painstaking observations seriously.

I succeeded in winning the boy's confidence simply by expressing a technical interest in his methods of data acquisition and analysis. This was the only thing that really mattered to him, and never before had he been able to share this consuming preoccupation with anyone.

Our first therapeutic sessions thus turned into a cram course in meteorology. This teen-age youngster proved so knowledgeable a teacher that I frankly felt I should be paying him a fee for a highly competent series of lectures. Yet when, in the course of therapy, I shifted the topic toward his personality problem, a curious change took place. The boy continued to deliver technical treatises on the weather, but his speech and his entire bearing became suffused with visible signs of deep, neurotic anxiety.

His speech became so rapid as to be unintelligible, it was compulsive in tone; and the word forms seemed altered (though his articulation was so fast that it was impossible to analyze them).

I recorded samples of the boy's speech during these nearly manic episodes and gave the tapes to an electronically adept friend who built a small device that permitted me to slow down the tape without lowering the voice pitch. This method—now a fairly common technique of electronic information retrieval—revealed the boy's torrential mumbo jumbo to be an astounding amalgam of scientific and obscene words. Arcane terminology referring to the physics of the upper atmosphere, wind velocities, cyclonic patterns, and pressure gradients were broken up into individual syllables, and these syllables were interspersed with such expressions as "fuck," "shit," "prick," "cunt," and "ass." The total speech conformation, reeled off at a rate that only a marvellously adept tongue could achieve, might be described as a dirty weatherman's pig Latin.

It was the obscene content of this language that provided the main clinical clue for the therapy. As it developed, Bernie harbored intense hostility toward his parents. He had never openly expressed this hostility, but had withdrawn into his lonely scientific pursuits. Never had he used obscene language outright. Only within the shelter of his safe retreat, within the framework of scientific language, was he able to give vent to those obscene tokens of aggression that less scholarly youngsters might have uttered more freely.

His fixation on the weather was in itself significant. For the changing weather symbolically represented to the boy his own inner climate, and his interest in predicting the weather corresponded to his underlying need to be prepared for and protected from the anxieties he encountered in himself.

In the course of therapy, I was able to persuade the boy's parents, who up to that time had rigorously opposed his penchant for meteorology as part of his "sick" syndrome, to revise this attitude. They began to use Bernie's specialized interest as a meeting ground on which improved communication could be established. Before therapy, Bernie had had to rely on the public library for his studies. Now his father provided him with books of his own and even bought him some instruments for weather observation.

It worked wonders. When the boy's energies were no longer consumed in spiting his parents, he also became more open toward his schoolmates and teachers. Gradually, his preoccupation with meteorology changed in basic character from a destructive passion to a rewarding hobby. At this writing, Bernie's prognosis appears to be good. Although he has not yet succeeded in widening his interests much beyond the weather, it seems likely that he may eventually be able to do so. When that happens, he may yet establish normal relations with his age group. Meanwhile, at least, he gets passing grades in school.

In Chapter Three, I pointed to the use of sexual obscenity by adolescent boys as a means of denying and overcoming their Oedipal castration fears and asserting their own virility in defiance of the rival father. This is often a fairly serious syndrome, and when such Oedipal feelings are intensified by other resentments against the father, the resultant psychic disfigurement can be truly horrifying.

A recent case of this kind was widely reported in the New York newspapers in September 1966, when a group of boys aged twelve to fifteen set fire to several vagrants in the skid-row district around the Bowery.

There was no doubt that these acts were carefully premeditated, for it took the boys a long time to collect the needed incendiaries. Wandering from pump to pump among the gas stations of the Lower East Side, the boys drew a few drops from each dangling hose until they had filled several milk bottles with gasoline. They soaked

the heads of several bums sleeping in unattended doorways, gently and carefully pouring the gasoline on their
hair so as not to awaken them. Then they struck a match
to their handiwork and watched with undenied amusement their victims' heads bursting into flame while the
agonized bums, screaming in pain, dumbly scrambled to
their feet . . . living torches.

My job, as court-appointed psychiatrist, was to probe
for a possible motive behind this seemingly senseless
crime. My first clue, characteristically, was one boy's aggressive obscenity. Even during the psychiatric interviews he berated me with a ceaseless stream of the crudest invective.

As it turned out, it was this particular boy who had
instigated the cremation. He was the one who had sold
the others on the enterprise, describing the anticipated
details in graphic and exciting terms. The other boys, having been promised a good show, just went along.

This boy, characteristically, was the only one who remained calm when confronted with a surviving victim.
The sight of the burned man, whose flesh had been seared
from his face, exposing patches of bare bone, was so
ghastly that some of the boys tried to run out of the room.
Yet the boy who had been the leader remained unmoved.

Gradually, this boy's personality unfolded in our interviews, and, in terms of his tragically distorted outlook,
the apparently senseless act assumed a grotesque logic.
The root of the matter was that the boy regarded his
father as a "bum" and hated him with unspeakable intensity.

The father had deserted his family, and the boy, conditioned by his Italian environment to place a premium on family loyalty, equated the concept of "deserter" with the concept of "dirty bum." The hostility was thus transferred from the father to bums in general and especially to dirty ones lying in doorways.

To make matters worse, the father, prior to absconding, had beaten the boy so cruelly as to cause a severe fracture. That such a boy would resort to obscenity as a general style of expression seems only natural in the light of the psycho-dynamics explained earler. It was a way of getting back at his father and of breaking any remaining bond of identification with him.

In this particular case, however, foul words were not enough. Something else had to be done to express the measure of this boy's rage. He literally had to burn his father—the bum—alive. And he did. To a person blind with hate, one man is as good—or as bad—as another.

One curious factor emerged from my interviews with this boy. By his own emotional logic, he felt a kind of moral imperative toward this vengeance, even though his victims were patently innocent of any wrong done to him. In burning the bums he was, in his own way, obeying a moral dictate.

It would be grossly incorrect, however, always to equate obscenity in youngsters with latent aggression. In groups which, aside from being functionally illiterate, are simply not verbally oriented, children often fail to develop normal speech skills. For them, obscenity becomes the sole area of communication.

I recall a striking illustration of this in a Danbury, Connecticut, movie theater, where I had gone to see the rerun of an old Humphrey Bogart film. The row of seats behind me had been invaded by a small band of Negro children, apparently from a cultural environment in which the use of language was, at best, marginal. Communication between them was partly accomplished through the tactile sense, the exchanges taking various forms ranging from playful boxing to hard blows or from teasing and rubbing to mutual masturbation. All through this rapid and intense touch activity they kept up a running commentary on the happenings on the screen. This commentary took the form of inarticulate yelps punctuated by two recurrent monosyllables—"fuck" and "shit." I could not help but admire the musical variety of intonations by which they invested these meager and drab syllables with a whole range of expressive content. From two syllables, they created a kind of language to reflect the various situations in the film.

The significant aspect of this is partly that these children apparently had no effective means of verbal communication except obscenity. But equally important is the fact that the meaning of the same utterance varied widely and was defined in each instance by its phonetic rather than its literal aspect. This constitutes an illiterate language outside of the basic use of the word—one that cannot be notated in letters.

It is hardly surprising that, in culturally underdeveloped groups, the pattern of speaking mainly in obscenities often carries over into adulthood. Even a person who, by dint of native intelligence, has risen above the limitations of such a group and attained the use of a greater portion of the language, sometimes reverts to obscene monosyllables under emotional stress. Such a case was mentioned to me by Colonel Herbert Hoff, who for many years served as psychiatrist in the U. S. Army. A private soldier with a service history of general competence and merit had, under the stress of front-line action in Korea, developed an emotional disturbance which reduced his vocabulary to a single word: "shit."

Curiously, the patient remained cooperative—even deferential—during the examination and answered questions as best he could with his one word. Again, inflection and gesture determined in each case what he meant by "shit." At one time it might mean, "Yes, indeed, very much so." At another time it might mean, "Absolutely no." On seeing a hypodermic syringe before an injection, "shit" clearly expressed his fear of the needle. And during a special Thanksgiving dinner prepared at his hospital, the word "shit" meant something like "compliments to the chef," clearly conveying his delight at having something good to eat.

While systematic exploration in this area is still in its beginning, the psychiatric understanding of obscenity in children, I believe, can be significantly deepened by taking into account some of the archetypal images and beliefs that are relatively more prominent in the minds of children than in those of adults, whose archetypal heritage is often displaced by cultural conditioning.

Until now, psychologists have tended to regard obscenity in children as a purely operational device—an instrument for manipulating adults. It was assumed that children were largely unaware of the subtle and sometimes profound overtones of archetypal taboo attached to such words. But in a highly perceptive monograph published in 1966, the eminent Dutch psychiatrist Joost A. M. Merloo, now practicing in New York, points to a deeper aspect of children's scatology. He traces the use of dirty words by children to an atavistic and almost universally shared belief in what he calls "anal magic."

We have already explained how a child uttering a scatologic word symbolically shits on the person to whom he speaks. If we admit the concept of anal magic, this act expresses something far deeper than mere spite or annoyance. Shitting on somebody has a profound atavistic meaning. It is an evil charm, inexorable and deadly.

Pursuing the roots of this atavism, I recently spoke with Robert Gannon, a journalist friend who had just returned from the jungles of Surinam, where he reported on "Operation Gwamba," a project to rescue animals from an area to be flooded by an artificial lake. In the course of this work, Mr. Gannon worked with a group of bush Negroes, descendants of escaped African slaves who established isolated jungle villages, quite distinct and separate from those of the native South American Indians. In these isolated settlements, ancient African myths and folkways have been preserved remarkably intact; and it soon became evident to Mr. Gannon that belief in anal magic was still strong among these tribes.

The bush Negroes proved themselves brave, gentle, and

adept in all phases of animal capture except one. They showed a seemingly unaccountable fear of animals that had climbed into trees. The reason for their reluctance to go after treed beasts was that these animals, either in terror or as a natural defense, often defecated on the men coming after them. Invariably, this produced panic and despair on the part of the befouled rescuer. The men appeared genuinely stricken with horror, and neither reassurance from the white expedition leader, nor the quick removal of the offending offal could console them. Not only did the beshitted men remain despondent for many hours, but fellow tribesmen often taunted them for their misfortune.

Only after the supervisor of the expedition had gained the friendship and confidence of his crew did the bush Negroes confide the reason for their horror. Quite aside from shunning the evident unpleasantness of being dirtied, they believed that the animal's excrement carried an evil spell, that it was a tangible malediction, an anal curse. No recourse availed the man on whom it fell.

Excremental taboos of this kind are common in many cultures. Indeed, they seem to permeate the instinctual life of the entire human species. When the biochemical mechanism of instinct is better understood, modern genetics may yet uncover the DNA link by which children and savages, in whom archetypal awareness has not yet been displaced by culturally imposed sophistication, hark back to the fundamental magic of inherited taboo.

Very likely the child feels subconsciously that, in shitting on another person, he takes possession of that person and thus gains control over him, in much the same way that a dog feels he acquires property rights to territory marked with his urine. Certain types of anal obscenity in children may be regarded as a symbolic substitute for such magic shitting.

Recognizing the element of primitive magic in children's scatology also throws new light on a syndrome that is extremely distressing to parents: children's swearing in church.

It is by no means uncommon to find children mumbling obscenities during religious services. My own informal observation, confirmed by other psychiatrists with whom I have discussed this matter, is that the incidence of compulsive obscenity in church is proportional to the degree of ritualization in the sacred service. Thus, for example, more such cases may be found among Catholics or orthodox Jews than among Unitarians. Essentially, the child is reacting to the mysterious forces so impressively invoked by the priest or rabbi. To assert and maintain his own identity in the face of powerful presences, such as those of priests and divine spirits, he recites his own magic words—the obscenities—as a sort of counter-litany, an infantile Black Mass.

Because self-assertion against fearful and mighty spirits is the common motivation for these obscene tirades, it stands to reason that the child feels compelled to make his utterance loud enough to be properly heard. This syndrome is usually uncontrollable prior to psychiatric treatment. Punishment or threats may create severe emotional trauma and secondary reinforcement of the disturbance.

While spiritual self-assertion is the usual motivating factor of such behavior, I have encountered children who utter obscenities in church for purely practical reasons. They simply want to try out the power of the dirty words.

Once a dirty word is acquired and recognized as a potential weapon, it must of course be tested. Normally, these tests are carried out in the home with parents or other familiar adults as prime targets. Yet the esthetically or spiritually sensitive child exposed to regular church attendance soon perceives that institutional dealings with God are fraught with precisely the kind of archetypal spells (here called prayers) to which his new interest in magic words has alerted him. With the innocent realism of the very young, he sees that the church is the most suitable arena for the kind of experiment he wants to conduct. In an operational field trial for his new weapons he is pitting magic against magic. By mumbling his obscene counter-litany in church, he opposes the powers of depravity to the powers of holiness, thereby testing both.

In one form or another, nearly every child conducts such a test at some stage in his life. Essentially, it is a test of social *vs.* individual values. Through the institutions of church and school, he begins to sense the vast scope of social forces. Often they overwhelm him by their magnitude. His defense is to oppose the ritual of obscenity to the ritual of social orthodoxy. It is his revolt against the whole world of ethical values with which society—represented by church and school—constrains the natural animalistic values of the child.

Repentance and submission, arising from the notion of

sin, along with a whole string of hateful orthodoxies in both the spiritual and civil realm, are forcibly imposed on the child by authoritarian adults. Parents, priests, and teachers usually induce fear and anxiety in their efforts to subjugate the child's mind and spirit to the dictates of our civilization. He must fight back to preserve at least a fragment of his natural identity. And quite often, his little black litany is his only armor against society's suffocating onslaught on his emergent self.

Parents with strict religious convictions are usually horrified at what seems to them a particularly shocking form of irreverence in their children, the irony of the situation being that the stricter the parents' religious outlook, the more likely their children's obscene apostasy. Often the parents fear that the child is literally damning himself beyond the theological limits of grace. For most religions stipulate repentance as a precondition of such grace and subsequent forgiveness and salvation. Yet when you talk to an obstreperous youngster of repentance, you merely strengthen his defiance. The very fact that you—an adult —are showing serious concern is proof that his dirty magic is really working. Your remonstrance emboldens him. You merely drive him on toward what, according to the Gospel, is the one unforgivable sin: blasphemy.

Faced with this situation, parents, not long ago, assumed their children to be bewitched and went scouting among their neighbors hunting for the witch. No doubt it is a measure of progress that nowadays they are more likely to consult, or be referred to, a psychiatrist.

My concern in such cases is as much with the parents

as with the child. I try to explain to the parents that the child is neither willfully sinning nor in thrall to some deliberately evil force. It is merely that the concept of salvation, whether clerically or socially defined, has no meaning to the child. He considers himself perfectly all right as he is. Hence he rejects any institutional attempt to infringe on his selfhood and mold him to the precepts of a dogma. The symptoms usually cease if the child is no longer exposed to religious ritual and pressure.

Avoidance of religion, of course, is hardly a satisfactory course to religiously oriented parents. I therefore point out to such parents that, after a period of relaxing religious instruction, they may begin again more successfully by trying to make religious values meaningful to the child in his own terms. Of course, this usually can be done only after the child is old enough to deal with certain abstract concepts. Moreover, it can be done only if the parent himself has a personal and essentially non-dogmatic understanding of the values underlying his religion.

The large number of clinical examples cited in this chapter should not implant the notion that children's use of obscenity always betokens an emotional disturbance. In certain age groups, the use of sexual as well as scatological obscenity may be regarded as entirely normal. During the so-called latency period, for example, which covers the age group from about eight to eleven years, children generally use dirty words as a substitute for actual sexual experimentation.

The use of four-letter words as sexual surrogates may be regarded as wholesome and even beneficial in this age

131

group. Because cultural restrictions in western society demand the delay of sexual activity in children, severe repressions might result if dirty words were not available to take the place of physical exploration in an area that increasingly occupies any normal child's interest. During this phase of psychosexual development, which is shared by both boys and girls, the use of the obscene words is generally confined to the youngster's own in-group.

Later, during puberty, when both boys and girls begin to engage in primitive erotic exploration among their playmates, the use of dirty words within the group generally declines and their subjective importance to the child diminishes.

Most middle-class parents, however, find it difficult to remain casual about their children's obscenity, and, as a psychiatrist, I am constantly faced with the parental question, "But doctor, what can I do?"

Probably the worst thing any parent can do is to forbid the child to use four-letter terms while he himself continues to use them. This inconsistency confuses children and undermines their confidence in the parent. In homes of lower cultural levels, where four-letter words are freely used, this often presents a problem.

The parent should, by quiet questioning, ascertain whether the child's use of four-letter language is part of a normal sexual maturation pattern, as discussed above, or perhaps purely imitative parroting of terms heard from playmates. Neither case calls for corrective measures.

However, if the child's obscenity appears to be accompanied by specific hostility against one or both parents, such language may be an indication of an incipient schizophrenia-like development. Psychiatric attention is definitely indicated in such cases, especially when the use of obscene words is accompanied by other forms of "obscene" behavior, such as indecent exposure, and signs of an underlying thought disorder.

A recent case of this type involved a fourteen-year-old girl. Highly intelligent and gifted, she was an excellent student at one of New York City's best high schools. Quite suddenly, and without any prior history of obscenity, the girl started using foul language and failing in most of her subjects.

The sudden emergence of this syndrome should have alerted the parents that the girl was probably suffering some kind of decompensatory emotional process. But the parents, partly from indifference and partly from procrastination, did little more than pretend to ignore their daughter's alarming new speech habits. This casual permissiveness proved a mistake, for it deprived the girl of the attention that she evidently craved in her disturbed condition.

The girl made sure that her next stop in her symbolic bid for attention would not be ignored. She undressed herself in school, during a class period, fighting off everyone who tried to restrain her until, stark naked, she harangued her transfixed audience with a hair-curling recital of obscenities. Immediate hospitalization was unavoidable.

In most instances, however, a reasonable talk between the child and one of his parents is all that is required to keep the child's obscenity from going out of control. In a middle-class milieu, the parent might explain realistically the special functions of such language, that it serves to express anger or disgust in certain situations, but should not be used inappropriately. Middle-class children often have very keen status feelings which parents may enlist to their aid. Several parents have told me that one of the most effective ways to stop spiteful obscenity on the part of otherwise non-neurotic children is to warn the child that obscenity simply makes him lose prestige. Even snobbery, it seems, can be made socially constructive.

7. Dirty Scrabble on the Couch

The pivotal figure in T.S. Eliot's *The Cocktail Party* is Sir Henry Harcourt-Reilly, a psychiatrist of sorts. One of his patients, after being touched on a sensitive spot of his ego, remonstrates: "I did not come here to be insulted."

Sir Henry replies: "You've come where the word 'insult' has no meaning."

True enough, the therapeutic relationship is, or should be, an oasis of frankness. The object is to shut off, at least temporarily, the outer environment, where the need for social role-playing often distorts thought and feeling. This suspension of the usual social demands in therapy also brings about a change in language, the medium through which therapy operates. Freed from conventional restrictions, language sheds its inhibitions at certain stages of a successful therapy. In the privileged enclave of the consulting room, insult, however vile or obscene, does not have the meaning it has in ordinary situations. But to say, as does Eliot, that insult has *no* meaning misses the point.

Quite to the contrary, a special diagnostic significance

135

attaches to the calculated "insults" by which the therapist may attempt to penetrate the ego defenses of a patient. Even more revealing is the spontaneous abuse often hurled by the patient at his doctor, for they indicate that transference—essential to the therapeutic relationship—is being established. And, most importantly, the therapist must evaluate a patient's obscenities as tokens of hostility directed at key figures and relationships, past or present.

My eminent colleague Dr. Theodor Reik speaks of the analyst's need to develop a "third ear" for the subtleties of a patient's expressions. My contention is that the "third ear" might also be profitably trained on the patient's unsubtleties. Grossness of language is not necessarily directness. Even the crudest obscenities are sometimes circuitous in terms of the patient's true expressive intent. Indeed, the obscenity itself may be part of his defensive armor, designed to throw the probing therapist off the track rather than guide him to the focus of the emotional disturbance. In short, obscenity on the analytic couch can be a kind of dirty scrabble—an intricate word game. Directly or indirectly, the pattern of this game reflects crucial aspects of the patient's syndrome.

Obscene words enable the patient to recapture the emotional tone of certain episodes that may have been significant in forming his maladjustment. My own observations confirm Ferenczi's classic statement that "delicate allusions to sexual processes and scientific and foreign designations for them do not have [the same emotional effect] as the words taken from the original popular erotic vocabulary of one's mother tongue." I have found that a patient may seem emotionally distant from crucial events in his own life when he talks about these events in neutral terms, but readily reveals his traumatic reaction to these incidents if he can be made to tell them in the plainer vocabulary of his childhood. Significant areas of conflict, which otherwise might have remained obscure, are often illuminated by obscene outbursts and can then be more fully explored.

The revelatory four-letter words, however, must be offered by the patient of his own accord. To lead a patient toward obscenity during a therapeutic session in hopes of releasing his emotional blocks often nullifies the diagnostic advantage the therapist might hope to gain. If the therapist deliberately (even though indirectly) encourages the patient to say "dirty things," obscene words will come too easily and will be uttered without the therapeutically relieving emotional discharge. The patient must be allowed to locate and work through his emotional blocks by himself.

An excellent paper by Dr. Marvin J. Feldman published some years ago in the *American Journal of Psychoanalysis* made the point that the diagnostic value of obscenities in therapy depends greatly on their timing. Ideally, they should be uttered at a stage of therapy where intuitive rapport has been established between analyst and patient and at a time when the patient has become fully convinced that the therapeutic situation is basically friendly and permissive and that he will neither be punished nor disapproved of no matter what he says.

From a diagnostic viewpoint, the complete avoidance

of obscenity in some patients can be as instructive to the therapist as uncontrolled outbursts are in others. If a patient subconsciously censors direct expressions of an anal or sexual nature, it is an almost certain sign of severe and far-reaching repressions and resistance to the therapeutic process.

I encountered an almost classic case of this type in a charming and lively girl in her early twenties, who, though otherwise functioning normally, was troubled by her compulsive need to reject all suitors. This rejection, by the way, did not take the form of avoiding men. On the contrary, she charmed them to pieces during the first stages of courtship, the better to dash their hopes in the end. In short, this seemingly warm and engaging creature was a compulsive castrater.

It was no surprise to discover that there had been a traumatic sexual encounter earlier in her life. That, after all, is the usual history of man-hating women. What intrigued me was her apparent inability to find any suitable language to describe the event. This was a highly significant clue. As it turned out, the girl's troubles stemmed less from having been (more or less) raped than from her inability to admit this fact either to herself or to others.

The incident, as I gradually gathered, took place in an Ivy League setting during a football weekend, after a prolonged necking session that had gotten out of control. Apparently she put up some resistance to the final intimacy, so that the occurrence might be technically classified as rape. But to her, rape was a four-letter word. She couldn't say it. She had to find some other way of telling what happened.

Coyly she said: "He touched all three bases."

I asked for some explanation but got only embarrassed, fidgety silence. Only after much insistent, though delicate, questioning was I able to elicit the information that the "three bases" were her breasts and genitals.

Not yet being certain just what happened, I asked: "He just touched them?"

The girl spun around, indignant at my blatant ignorance of baseball. "Oh no," she protested. "He scored a home run!"

I couldn't help but smile at the irony of hearing the deeply traumatized girl describe her defloration so sportingly. Yet this was the vital clue to the crabbed tangle of her repressions. The fact that intercourse had taken place didn't particularly distress her. Like most modern girls, she did not invest defloration with the cataclysmic importance that earlier generations bestowed on it. What bothered her more than anything else was that she hadn't planned on its happening just then. She was an orderly, organized, purposeful person. Losing her virginity by oversight, as it were, just wasn't her style. And that rankled.

To restore her self-esteem, she constructed an elaborate syndrome of repressions. Not only was admitting the crucial event ruled out; even the basic vocabulary describing it became taboo to her. By resorting to baseball terminology, she was, in effect, employing a kind of inverse obscenity—a nice-Nellyism sharing the same psychological roots as true obscenity.

It occurred to me later that her choice of the term "home run" seemed singularly apt, in Freudian symbology, for the young man's importune foray into uterine environs. But such speculations probably transgress the sometimes hazy borderline between medicine and poetry.

While the concept of obscenity was *im*plicit in the language of the "baseball fan," *ex*plicit obscenity often occurs in psychiatric sessions on the part of persons with an obsessive need for self-depreciation.

Probably the most foul-mouthed patient I ever treated was a young professor of philosophy who almost incessantly swore at himself. He did this not merely on the analytic couch, but also at home, particularly in the privacy of the bathroom when faced with his mirror image while shaving. Whenever Mark couldn't keep up his stream of obscene self-abuse, as in public situations, he suffered from a stubborn stammer. This impaired his effectiveness as a lecturer and threatened to cut short an otherwise promising academic career.

An allied problem was the man's painful shyness in all social situations, including interviews with his students. So overwhelming were his feelings of personal insufficiency that he felt himself to be an impostor in his role as teacher. Counseling students in private conferences was sheer hell to him. He was appalled at what he felt to be his arrogance in presuming to offer advice to a student. To punish himself for this imagined arrogance, he would bolt for the toilet after each interview to tell himself loudly before the mirror, "I'm just a rotten, stinking shithead."

The self-descriptions he used in the analytic sessions were considerably more colorful, and I was constantly astonished at the transformation of his personality during these obscene tirades. The normally shy, withdrawn man assumed a masterful attitude, an air of truculent authority during these spasms of self-castigation. He was quite literally not himself. As analysis later showed, he assumed the identity of his own father in these episodes.

Mark had grown up as the son of a traveling salesman in a lower-middle-class Jewish family. As a precocious child, he had shown an early interest in intellectual pursuits. This infuriated his father, an aggressively stupid man, painfully conscious of his limitations, who refused to be intellectually upstaged by his young son. As the father couldn't answer most of the questions asked by the bright child, he would, in reply, let loose a stream of obscene invective against the pesky boy.

The primary purpose of these crudities was to belittle the boy's intelligence, thus making the father's own position in the family more secure. "You got shit in your head" and "Your mouth is bigger than your asshole" were standard retorts to whatever the boy said. But the scope of the abuse soon widened beyond recriminations against the boy's intellectual curiosity. Heaping verbal dirt on the child, the father made the boy feel like an intruder in his own home.

Curiously, the mother—in the submissive manner of a traditional old-world Jewess—did not protect her small son from the paternal rage. Mark never forgave her. His contempt for his mother equalled his hate for his father.

At last, Mark got rid of them both—or thought he did. Harshly rigorous self-discipline as much as native intelligence helped him toward the academic distinctions and scholarships that were the foundation of his career. As soon as he could support himself through a minor university post, he left home and has not spoken to any member of his family since.

But no man can shed his parentage. His mother pursued Mark through his attitude toward other women. He was pathetically afraid of them. If his own mother had betrayed him, what woman could he trust?

His father also pursued him in absentia. When the father was no longer present to berate him, he incorporated and introjected the function of the father into his own personality: part of him became the insulting father, and he started berating himself.

Throughout his life, Mark had been motivated by a quiet rage against his father. But, after fleeing from his father, he found that he could not function without him. He needed him as a scourge to sustain the intellectual vitality that had helped him toward his academic distinctions and was now making him, despite his difficulties, one of the most stimulating teachers on the faculty of his university. Consequently, he had to resort to those I-am-my-father episodes in which he shouted obscene abuse at himself to whip up his own level of motivation while using stammering in the presence of others as an unconscious defense against verbal self-abuse in public.

At the outset of therapy, Mark's obscene outbursts against himself were uncontrollable. But as he gained insight into the connection between his own obscenities and those his father had hurled at him, it became possible for him to cut short these outbursts by a rigorous application of this insight. Thanks to his outstanding intelligence —the chief integrating force in his personality—his prognosis now seems excellent. The stammer, though still present at this time, is less severe, and he is able to accomplish much of his work without depending on self-denigration as a motivational stimulus as well as a sado-masochistic punitive device.

Obscene self-description is fairly common among women with sexual conflicts or uncertainties. Women who, for whatever reason, find it difficult to form satisfactory love relationships sometimes try to assert their sexuality through obscene talk. Typically such women believe that men do not think of them as persons but merely as "cunts." In their more self-destructive moments they accept this evaluation of themselves and act accordingly.

Ingeborg, for example, had all the attributes of a great lady. At twenty-five, she had the grace and poise most women achieve only long after the bloom of youth, if ever. Hauntingly beautiful she was—and I well remember the lean symmetry of her face and the fawnlike fragility of her frame. Add to this a high level of intelligence, an excellent education, and social connections in fashionable artistic circles in New York and Zurich, and you have the picture of an exquisite and exceptionally sophisticated personality. Yet Ingeborg thought of herself simply as a sex machine.

The main symptoms of her difficulty were her inability to form any meaningful and lasting attachments and her tendency to make up in sheer numbers what her relationships lacked in quality.

Her language in therapy sessions reflected much of her attitude toward herself. Returning from a brief vacation in Jamaica, she told me of her encounter with "Vic the Prick"—a man she picked up on the street and knows by no other name. Naturally, Vic made the most of his opportunities. As Ingeborg puts it, "I really put him through my wringer." She always pictures herself as the aggressor in sexual encounters.

Vic, it seems, was put through a sort of endurance test of various sexual exercises, which included such exhausting maneuvers as "shooting him down in flames." By the middle of the second day, Vic excused himself to go out for cigarettes, promising to be back soon. He never returned. Ingeborg's resentment at being stood up turned against herself: "I'm just a big fucking hole with my clit hanging out!"

Her trouble began in late adolescence when her uncle, a successful lawyer, started continually propositioning her. Under such circumstances, a girl might find emotional reassurance in a meaningful relationship with her parents. But in Ingeborg's case, the estranged mother was always abroad, and her father—a well-known artist—had the disconcerting habit of bursting into the bathroom to ogle her in the shower.

Ingeborg, in short, had no refuge from her own attractiveness. That men chased her seemed natural enough; but that even her uncle and her father were after her threw things out of perspective. For her, this incestuous pursuit put normal love relations out of the question. So she turned about and—as a kind of revenge—started chasing the men, for which she was superbly equipped. To make her revenge complete, she tried to dispense with men altogether and dabbled for a while in lesbianism.

But she didn't really hate women, so it was no fun—after all, it was men she wanted to get even with. She made herself into an impersonal "fuck machine" so that men—who so much desired her—could never possess her. Ingeborg the cunt was put at everyone's disposal so that Ingeborg the person would remain out of the reach of all outsiders.

But the stratagem backfired. Ingeborg the person eventually moved out of reach of even Ingeborg herself. As her language indicated, all that remained, even in her own view, was Ingeborg the cunt.

Up to a point, Ingeborg's therapy has been successful. At least it has saved her from those wilder excesses that might have seriously endangered her safety. But every time she is on the verge of reintegrating her sexuality with the rest of her personality, she takes fright, breaks off the therapy, and runs off to a fashionable resort for some new exploit in depersonalized sex. A few weeks later she usually shows up in New York again, begging me to accept her once more as a patient. At this time, I cannot yet formulate a prognosis in this case. But in her frank declaration, "I'm just a big fucking hole with my clit hanging out," Ingeborg has certainly described her status quo with precision and candor. The pungency of her language is in itself a hopeful sign. The very violence of her self-disgust may precipitate a positive breakthrough in her therapy.

I have cited the foregoing cases because they represent fairly direct relationships between the psychodynamic nature of the underlying conflict and the patient's mode of expression. In many instances, however, the link between four-letter words uttered in therapy and the patient's focal trauma is far more circuitous and complicated. To trace this connection, the analyst may classify obscenities according to three basic types: oral, anal, and phallic. This typology of four-letter words corresponds to the level of regression to which the patient has returned, in the face of intolerable stress. Each of these three types of obscenity correlates with certain unconscious motivational factors in the patient.

Categorizing obscenities into oral, anal, and phallic groups provides a basic compass by which the analyst may gain preliminary orientation in the strange territory of the patient's neurosis.

To the analyst, a patient's pattern of obscenity is a special code—a four-letter word game in the sense that mathematicians use the term "game" to describe arbitrary coding patterns and the manipulation of symbols. In emotional disorders, a large segment of the patient's total language is encoded into a system of nearly impenetrable private meanings. But, unlike a purely verbal or a simple mathematical code, neurotic expression is multidimensional. The purely verbal aspect is interwoven through many layers of the patient's total personality structure. Four-letter words, because of their emotional depth effect, sometimes lay bare hidden areas of the patient's personal symbology, revealing some of the interlocking features of his neurotic or psychotic concept system and his defensive operations. In sum, four-letter words are handy tools for therapeutic code-cracking.

The mechanism of regression plays a key part in the interpretation of obscenity. Each person acquires specific forms of behavior by cultural conditioning. These largely determine how he functions in his interpersonal relationships and in a larger societal context. Yet frequently he harbors a suppressed wish to get rid of these culturally imposed modes of feeling. The more "civilized" he is, the more his instinctual patterns have been subjugated to the demands of his culture, the more he is likely to feel a subconscious urge to cast off his cultural conditioning and return to some kind of elemental spontaneity. In doing so, he dimly senses, he might regain those creative wellsprings within him that are the source of a transcendent feeling of being alive.

The exceptional person attains this kind of spontaneity within an acceptable setting—of creative work, of love, or some kind of sainthood. Many attain it only within the deceptive framework of alcohol, drugs, neurosis or crime. And some attain this precious instinctual spontaneity by becoming obscene. For the latter, obscenity is a verbal regression to a more primitive, less circumscribed, and seemingly more secure level in their social and psychosexual development.

From the standpoint of analytic therapy, the particular obscenities chosen by a patient reflect the level of his regression. A person regressing all the way back to the *oral* phase betrays the nature of his disturbance by employing predominantly oral forms of obscenity along with such oral manifestations as biting, sucking, gluttony, and token gestures of cannibalism. Narcissistic neuroses, manic psychoses, melancholia, and autoerotic preoccupations and delusions are often signalled by frequent use of orally oriented terms.

In contrast, obsessive-compulsive neuroses, paranoia, and paranoid conditions represent the terminal states of regression to the *anal* phase. Such disorders often lead to obscene language of the anal-sadistic kind. Finally, a person regressing to the *phallic* level, represented in various forms of hysteria, may resort to phallic obscenities centering on the penis or clitoris as well as on castration and Oedipal images.

It is difficult to describe these complex psychodynamics without resorting to the technical vocabulary of psychoanalysis. Rather than pursue this discussion on the abstract level, it may be better to cite case histories that, at least in some aspects, exemplify the principles involved.

At fifty, Mr. B. was an executive in a firm importing special metallurgical equipment. His department had been successfully marketing a Swedish flame-hardening machine, but for some years growing domestic competition had been cutting sharply into business. As sales slipped, he, being in a key position, somehow felt personally responsible for the decline. Faced with the possibility that his firm might scuttle his department, he became unreasonably distressed and anxious. Though his job was not directly endangered—he would have been transferred to another department—he became increasingly depressed and unable to concentrate. He forgot appointments and often stayed away from the office while wandering aimlessly in the streets. Growing more and more apathetic, he finally did not even want to get up in the morning. His wife had to menauver him out of bed, and urge him to get shaved and dressed; and ultimately he became so dependent on her that she practically had to feed him.

At this stage, not being able to face reality, he had apparently regressed to the level of a helpless infant. During therapy, the oral level of his regression was also indicated by food-oriented, semi-obscene expressions. "Rotten" was his favorite adjective. He frequently declared that he couldn't "stomach" something and was always threatening to "puke." After about two months he developed various physical gastric symptoms, including the habit of loud and compulsive belching.

Again, this is an exceptionally clear-cut case. More often, the signal words are less obvious. But nearly all cases of oral regression express themselves in alimentary metaphors or actions. Gluttony is often part of this syndrome, and, as might be expected, patients of this type are especially prone to alcoholism. In general, oral regressions result in manic-depressive symptoms and the simpler forms of schizophrenia. As a group, they are characterized by extremely immature behavior.

Mr. B., by the way, made a spontaneous recovery when another importer—aware of the decline of his product but unaware of his personal decline—offered him a job. His pride, which had been so undermined, was quickly restored by the new challenge. After a brief recuperative period, Mr. B. plunged himself into his new duties and soon was able to terminate this therapy. In a society dominated by commercial values, it is perhaps not too surprising to find a man's ego hitched to a sales curve.

The compulsive neuroses characteristically associated with anal regression reflect themselves in references to shit of all sorts—horseshit, bullshit, and plain shit. Words like "ass," "crappy," and "stinking" predominate in the anal repertoire. Hoarding of various types, from collecting Matisse to stacking old newspapers, often accompanies anal regression. Persons of this type nearly always have a larder full of canned goods. A favorite adjective is "dirty." In positions of authority, such persons often treat subordinates as "dirt." They are likely to use the word in reference to ethnic minorities in expressions such as "dirty Jew" or "dirty spic." Racial bigotry is rampant among the anally oriented.

As an inverse manifestation of his subconscious anality and preoccupation with dirt, the compulsive-neurotic is often meticulously neat. Order and neatness, both in his personal grooming and in his surroundings, often take on a ritual compulsive aspect. As one of my patients put it, "One must always be ready for inspection."

The most complex neuroses or psychoses are often those associated with the phallic phase; for such cases the syndrome becomes established at a relatively mature and highly organized conceptual level. One of my patients combined such a disorder with characteristically obscene speech patterns. A musician in his early thirties, he had just gained the beginnings of international fame when an airplane in which he was traveling had to make an emergency landing on fairly rough terrain. No one was seriously hurt, but the impact shook up the passengers rather badly. My patient suffered a slight concussion with no neurologic consequences. Physically he recovered completely.

Emotionally he was ruined. The fear of imminent death during the aircraft's perilous descent became the focal point of a rapidly developing psychosis. Having been, as it were, cheated of his physical death, he substituted symbolic death: he would not make music any more.

He insisted that he was unable to play, that he could no longer control his fingers. He replaced the considerable satisfactions of his former career with megalomanic fantasies. He kept telling me of imaginary concerts at which he sold out Carnegie Hall, of triumphant tours and best selling recordings. The tragic irony of it all lay in the fact that, before his mishap, all that he now invented had indeed been true.

Listening to his own recordings made before the accident, he would brim over with delight, proudly commenting on his technique and musicianship. Sometimes, in these elated moods, he would take his cello and run off dazzling passages with superb aplomb. Yet when faced with the prospect of playing again before an audience, his psychotic anxieties suddenly seized and literally paralyzed his hands. He blamed this paralysis on the injuries suffered in the accident, injuries that had long since healed. He would not admit or take account of the fact that, only moments before, he had played his instrument with full mastery of his former skill.

Personal importance, power, and influence were a predominant theme of his fantasies, and the theme was always stated with the bragging overemphasis that often masks underlying doubt.

It was during these blustering rodomontades that I became aware of his frequent use of phallic obscenities. No music critic was ever mentioned without a phallic prefix, and corporate entities, such as concert managements or the principal newspapers of New York, Chicago, London, and Amsterdam, were nearly always referred to as "those fuckers." This appeared all the more significant since I had been told by members of his family that the patient rarely, if ever, had used four-letter words in his conversation before the accident.

Not long after the phallic element in his psychosis had begun to show up more and more insistently in his speech, his focal anxiety clearly shifted from musical competence to sexual potency. The critics, he claimed, were trying to get him "by the balls"—a patently unwarranted statement in view of the favorable press he had enjoyed before his illness. Women, in his esteem, fared even worse than critics. Collectively, they were "ball-breakers," despite his formerly vigorous and generally happy sex life. Musical and sexual metaphors became curiously mixed. "Tuning up" was his term for erection. The perils of snapping strings or inadequate bow tension were preying on his mind and promptly projected into the sexual sphere. In this way he became pathetically concerned about the physical condition of his penis, which he symbolically associated with his fiddle.

It took over four years of therapy to restore this superbly talented man to the point where he could resume his career. While still under my care, he summoned the courage for a major concert, and the critical acclaim he received is now helping him stage a remarkable comeback, artistically as well as psychologically.

From the viewpoint of this discussion, it is worth noting that the patient's phallic obscenities gave an early clue to the phallic focus of his regression and suggested appropriate therapeutic steps.

In all the foregoing examples, patients used obscenity because they were trying to tell the therapist something they could not directly express. At times, however, obscenity is used for the opposite purpose—to erect a barrier between patient and therapist designed to shield the patient against what he feels to be a threatening situation. Because neurosis is in itself a protective device, most neurotics feel impelled, at least at the outset of therapy, to keep their neurosis intact at all costs.

I have had numerous experiences with patients who had acute anxieties about the process of therapy itself and vented their fear by berating me in an obscene and insulting way. Quite often their slurs were directed at my accent and my generally European manners. In a few cases this difficulty on the part of the patient in accepting my European origin was translated into a fantasy play of "guessing" at my true identity.

"You're not Dr. Hartogs," declared one patient, pointing an accusing finger. "You killed the real Dr. Hartogs, and now you are impersonating him."

He paused to let that one sink in. Then he slammed down his trump. "You are a Nazi criminal," he shouted. "Don't think I'll let you get away with it!" He burst into a string of obscenities, cursing me as a Nazi murderer all the more despicable for assuming my victim's identity.

On another occasion, a woman patient accused me amidst screams and obscene curses of being a sex criminal escaping the consequences of my misdeeds by posing as a psychiatrist.

In both these cases, the patients projected their own identity doubts and guilt feelings onto me, at the same time preventing me by their hostility from probing the structure of their delusions. Obscenity was used in the subconscious hope that it would poison the therapeutic relationship and thus cut short the treatment, leaving the pathological devices of the patient intact.

In both instances, fortunately, I was able gradually to gain acceptance by these patients. It is significant that the woman who accused me of sexual wrongdoing was a lesbian engaged in what is, at least culturally, a forbidden sex activity.

During the early sessions of her therapy she frequently restated her doubts as to my identity. What bothered her was the final "s" in my name, with its plural implications. "Hartogs," she mused out loud, "there must be two of you. And you're the phoney!"

This was a tip-off. Her own problem, it turned out, was

one of a personality built entirely on the concept of role-playing. She had no self-concept. Everything was make-believe, a kaleidoscope of perfunctory mimicries.

The trouble stemmed from the fact that her father never accepted her as his child. Suspecting some other paternity, he openly told her when she was still quite young, "You're a bastard. Your real father is an alley cat." So she grew up in two identities—outwardly a member of her household, but in her secret fantasy life an alley-cat off-spring with no true claim to her home. Later, when she had firmly settled into a lesbian pattern, her identity doubts so incapacitated her that she could no longer go out and face people. She felt her lesbianism—symbolically, her alley cat-ism, her outcastness—"shows in my eyes." She has since made a satisfactory recovery, enabling her to resume her work as a teacher.

As for the man who accused me of being a Nazi crim-inal and my own murderer, I learned that in his childhood his father had abandoned him, during the Nazi invasion of Belgium—an act which the boy always regarded as a "crime." In accusing me of being a criminal like his father he had, in effect, already laid the ground for my acting as a father surrogate—a fairly auspicious beginning for what proved to be a wholly successful therapy. At one point, after a stormy and vituperative session, he bolted from the consultation room, but did not leave my suite. Instead, he puttered around the waiting room, rearranging all the furniture. I instructed my receptionist to let the man do as he pleased and meanwhile received another patient. The man waited patiently until the other patient left.

Then he contritely returned to my office. "I hope you like the way I set up your furniture."

It was a pathetic but genuine bid for confidence and forgiveness. From that time on, he no longer berated me with his obscene outbursts. Soon afterward he even let me put the furniture back where it belonged.

The most stubbornly ingrained psychopathic patterns are often those involving compulsive muttering of obscenities without surcease. The *British Journal of Psychiatry* reported recently that an obstinate case of this kind was effectively cured by making the patient exaggerate his symptoms. He was asked to say the obscenities he could not control in "incessant and explosive repetition" as loud and fast as he could until he was exhausted. The purpose of this therapy was to build up the patient's own inhibitions against his symptoms.

Such a therapy, quite obviously, may relieve the embarrassing symptoms, but it is not likely to get at the deeper neurotic causes. Very likely the suppressed neurotic conflict will show up in another and perhaps more dangerous form.

I believe that conditions of this kind are characteristic of individuals suffering from a high degree of what Durkheim termed "anomie"—a profound alienation from the total cultural context. Such disorders, consequently, should be viewed not in narrow medical terms but in broad cultural perspective.

The rising incidence of such cases may be interpreted as a sign that our times are becoming culturally unstuck to an alarming degree. Individuals necessarily react to "the materials at hand" within their culture, to borrow an apt phrase from literary critic Webster Schott. Among the prevalent materials at present Schott lists "epidemic dislocation, conditioning to insanity, and reality beyond explication." Facing a reality beyond explication, it is little wonder that many of the more responsive individuals go beyond the bounds of reason under the pressure of irresolvable cultural contradictions. Not all of them can attain a necessary level of sophistication—a kind of inner distance from their own culture that lets them view the agonizing self-contradictions in the modern western world as an unavoidable by-product of rapid cultural change. When such persons experience acute personal stress on top of their cultural alienation, they are prone to so-called breakdowns.

Our time has been called the first post-Christian century. Old verities, formerly presumed to be like the Rock of Ages, have given way to the onslaught of a new technologic and commercial paganism. Science has scrambled the traditional picture of the world, with the new biology doing as much to upset established notions as Kepler's new astronomy did three centuries ago. Freudian and post-Freudian psychology have given man a new self-image more challenging but less flattering (and far less comforting) than the traditional view.

These changes, to be sure, are opening undreamed-of horizons for intellectual venture and personal achievement. But in the febrile atmosphere of fast cultural change, they all too often produce anxiety rather than stimulation. In the tumbling maelstrom of change, aims, ideals, and values become ambiguous, and the individual is no longer able to orient himself. His whole system of social coordinates has, if not collapsed, at least become bent into Einsteinian relativities.

Not all individuals can find a mode of psychologic survival under such conditions. Paradoxically, the educated, intelligent person—the person most aware of these cultural changes—suffers the least from them. The likelier victim is the man who dimly senses that his cultural guideposts are all askew but doesn't know why or how. Overcome with the vastness of changes and dislocations he cannot comprehend, perplexed by his personal troubles, and deprived of the sence of a sustaining community in impersonal urbanized settings, the unstable person often withdraws from it all into obscene expressions of private dissent. The little dirty words immediately resolve the clashing conflict, for the magic of their obscene spell equates all values. With grand impartiality, the dirty word, applied broadly to the whole world, makes everything come out even. All is equal to zero.

The echo of this melancholy equation persists at many levels. We hear it in the persistence of obscenity in contemporary fiction, drama, and avant-garde cinema. Unlike the invigorating force of genuine ribaldry, which I have welcomed in an earlier chapter, the drearily recurrent four-letter language in a lot of contemporary writing is but a mirror image—on another level—of the lonely derelict's obscene daydream. Both are resigned, defeatist expressions of our current cultural anarchy. Both are evasions of the greatest intellectual challenge ever afforded to any generation.

The haplessly muttering patient is indeed a pathetic dropout from the rough cultural curriculum of our time.

In his solipsistic isolation, obscenity becomes the last sustaining ritual, the only utterance that retains for him a shred of life's essence—the semblance of meaning.

Nonstop mumbling of obscenities is a nonspecific symptom and therefore difficult to interpret in terms of the more orthodox trauma-oriented psychiatric theories. Those leaning toward a more broadly philosophic point of view may envision such behavior as a category of existential despair. The patient is reduced to the primal utterance of curses because in his psychic situation other forms of language no longer offer any means of meaningful expression. Randomly scattered curses then represent a desperate attempt to fill an overwhelming emptiness.

Whether the ceaselessly cursing person senses this emptiness in himself or in the world surrounding him is, under those conditions, a moot point. If the world seems empty, so is the self.

For the same reason it is irrelevant whether such subjective emptiness is felt to exist in the world at large or in the language. For, if language becomes to him emotionally inadequate as a means of expression or communication, the result is human isolation as complete as if the world itself were vacuous.

Typically, the mumbled maledictions seem addressed to no one in particular. They are private notes elucidating an abysmal sense of combined inner and outer void.

Walter Kerr, in an essay on the work of Edward Albee, poses the question of the ultimate limits of language:

"What lies below language? Anything? Are there no tools of persuasion left?"

Kerr then comments on a father's effort to establish

contact with his estranged daughter in Albee's play *A Delicate Balance*: "With an effort of will and a noticeable anguish . . . some words might be found through which he and his daughter might meet . . . a 'breakthrough,' a kind of agony of communication might be achieved.

"Suppose he did break through, suppose he did succeed in breaking through the wall of meaningless sound that keeps husbands and wives and daughters and friends locked away from one another. Sentences might be formed that would breach the wall. . . . But *then* what would he say?

"The implication is that words can be fitted together well enough but that the moment they are, all substance vanishes. Struggling minds come together and after a hard tussle embrace—only to discover at the point of fusion that they are embracing empty air. Words are names for things that do not exist. Pressed hard enough, put together precisely enough, they at last touch nothing. With the end of each perfectly formed sentence, the universe runs out of breath."

More movingly than anything I have ever read, this passage suggests the world of utmost alienation—the world even beyond the solitary obscene curse—the world of those who see no alternative to suicide.

I have on occasion dealt with patients who have touched and gone beyond this outermost frontier. Yet, as a physician operating through the instrument of language, I am not prepared to discount its healing functions categorically. Though in my profession I can take no position on religious matters, I find myself more in accord with the German theologian Gerhard Ebeling of Tübingen University on the problem of language.

A word, Ebeling suggests, is not merely a means of conveying information; it is also a symbol of man's power over nature and thus useful in making the world a fit habitat for himself. In this sense, any word, any utterance —no matter how lowly or how obscene—is a banner of hope. And even the most self-absorbed muttering is a symbol of human community. Ultimately, no man can speak except to another.

8. Dirty Humor

Travel has occupied a good part of my life, and, among other souvenirs, I have gathered in my journeys a multinational collection of dirty stories. Professionalism, I admit, was happily mixed with curiosity in this kind of data acquisition; and I carried this baggage mostly in my mind, for otherwise it wouldn't have passed customs.

Prolonged sojourns in Germany and France, in particular, provided opportunities for sampling the more colorful jokes of these countries; and they leave no doubt that the Gallic temperament is indeed radically different from the Teutonic. If the notion of national character is ever questioned by a student of cultural anthropology, I strongly recommend some research in bars and locker rooms.

In comparing geographic regions in terms of their obscenities, I was long ago struck by the predominance of anal humor among the Germans. My first exposure to typically Teutonic merriment was a standing joke foisted on me by a German-born grade-school teacher in charge of my class in the little Dutch town where I grew up.

163

Like so many elementary-grade teachers in prewar Europe, he was essentially a repressed, bureaucratic person, the prototype of a small-time, small-town government clerk. He permitted himself only one departure from the punctilious. Whenever one of the little boys in his class audibly broke wind, he would interrupt himself in mid-sentence, point a finger heavenward, roll his eyes, and solemnly announce: "Aha! Methinks I hear the stentorian call of the arse-trombone!"

Whatever may have moved this frustated little man to perform his grotesque ritual whenever the occasion presented itself, he certainly did no harm thereby. Invariably, the class responded with howling laughter, deliberately prolonged to forestall resumption of the lecture. Rather than shock us into shame about our natural digestive functions, these gleeful classroom events merely encouraged us to more heroic efforts toward anal audibility.

Some of my erstwhile schoolmates, having learned to laugh at a bodily function that others perceived as a grim taboo, may have grown up to enjoy a generally untrammeled sensuality in their later years. The credit, paradoxically, belongs to my dusty little teacher, whose singular obscenity was very likely the only open window in an otherwise tightly shuttered life.

The impression he left on me must have been quite profound; for, long after I had left his school and, as a university student, developed a serious interest in music, his little joke would haunt me at most inappropriate times. In Mozart's *Requiem*, for example, the bass soloist invokes the trumpets of the Last Judgement with the great aria "Tuba Mirum." But my preconditioned mind somehow translated the Latin "tuba mirum" (literally: "marvelous trombone") into the kind of personal trombone I had practiced in my grade-school class. Invariably, it broke me up at one of Mozart's most magic moments, and my seat neighbors at the Concertgebouw in Amsterdam may have wondered what I was giggling about during the *Mass for the Dead*.

Later my psychoanalytic studies alerted me to the link between the predominant anality of German humor and the many shades of pedantry that lie at the root of the best and the worst in the German national character. It is, after all, the compulsive, painstaking thoroughness of anally oriented personalities that has given us the great intellectual achievements of German science and scholarship, along with the structured magnificence of a Bach fugue. Psychoanalytically speaking, it implies no disrespect to say that these are the works of men who took their toilet training seriously. Conversely, we might point to the spectacular formation drill of goose-stepping Nazis at the Nürnberg rallies, and ultimately to the ovens at Auschwitz and Buchenwald as manifestations of the same thoroughgoing anality, with its typically sadistic undertone.

The horrors that were to come from the enshrinement of anality as a national ideal through the mind and personality of Adolf Hitler were still unimagined and unthinkable during my student days. But even then the prevalence of certain anal crudities in the whole climate of expression foreshadowed the imminence of a disciplined, destructive authoritarianism.

Too often, on frequent visits to Germany, I would hear

the phrase ". . . or I'll bust your ass!" added gratuitously to orders or instructions. I also recall the astounding number of children's rhymes whose tag line relates the loss of bowel control—a hilarious event to the anally obsessed.

A similar level of anal humor was evident on the cover of a German magazine dating from about 1930, which I still remember distinctly. It showed a dachshund circumambulating a tree and encountering his own rear around the bend. Evidently unaware whose posterior he faces, he eagerly extends his nose. But the caption spells out his letdown: "Ach, it's only me!"

And surely it is no accident that the most famous quotation in all German literature was really never written out at all by the fastidious Goethe. He just put down three dots where the hero of his historical drama *Götz von Berlichingen* challenges an adversary to lick his arse. But wherever German is spoken, a brief reference to Goethe under appropriate circumstances clearly implies the same invitation. Without doubt, the bulk of Germany's population knows its great poet for this line alone.

The difference between German and French humor roughly corresponds to the difference between potato dumplings and crêpes Suzettes. The German joke usually makes its point with elephantine emphasis. The French joke, as likely as not, simply takes wing. These traits are shared alike by clean and dirty jokes.

By the time I had the opportunity to spend extended periods in France, I had already developed a professional ear for dirty stories and was all the more astonished at the paucity of anal jokes in France. To be sure, *"merde"* is ubiquitous, but paradoxically it carries no anal connotation in either the anatomical or the psychological sense. It implies nothing repressive, nothing loathsome. *"Merde,"* to the French, is simply a sort of one-syllable synopsis of the human condition. Depending on context, it may mean anything from a dispassionate, almost antiseptic, statement of annoyance to a sort of verbal good-luck charm. It has no place in dirty stories.

The main concern in Gallic off-color stories is the refinement and variation of sexual technique. Even the cruder jokes tend to stick to this theme. Sitting during the late hours in a rural bistro in the Burgundian wine county near Dôle, I—the sole stranger—was resolutely ignored by the vineyard workers assembled there. But I could not help overhearing the triumphant tag line of one of their stories: "I'm not impotent as long as I've got one finger left!"

Aside from its main focus on sexual technique, the French dirty joke concerns itself with such corollary subjects as cuckolding and the more amiable aspects of seduction. Amiability, in fact, is the key word in describing most French obscenities. This stands in marked contrast to their Anglo-Saxon equivalents, whose principal trait is one of nastiness and disguised aggression.

For the French, a subject may be obscene without being dirty, a distinction which the guilt-ridden Protestant mentality is largely incapable of making. In France, the idea of obscenity is akin not to filth but to the taking of forbidden pleasure and therefore is adumbrated not by feelings of lewdness but rather by an aura of naughty delight.

The repulsive element so deeply implicit in our notion of obscenity is almost wholly lacking. To the Anglo-American mind, it may seem almost a contradiction in terms to say that the main characteristic of a French off-color joke is its elegance.

The French seem to approach the subject of sex, in jokes and in general, with a *savoir faire* unparalleled in the western world. Only the ancient Chinese, to judge by their literature, achieved a similarly happy acceptance of the facts of life.

What accounts for this unique attribute of the French? Centuries of uninterruptedly high level of civilization may have contributed, especially since a strong vein of hedonism has always permeated the values of this civilization. The pleasures of good food, good drink, and beautiful works of art have penetrated more broadly and deeply into the fabric of the French nation than of any other. No wonder the pleasures of sex, and their expression in the form of jokes, unfold more gracefully in such an ambience. Even the rites of initiation—feared and sordid episodes in many other lands—take on a cheerful and pleasant rationality in France.

A medical colleague of mine, now practicing in New York, recalls how these things are done. During his student days at the University of Toulouse, he roomed in the house of an altogether respectable French family. One morning, on making his bed, the maid noticed traces of a nocturnal emission on the sheets—a fact she promptly reported to Madame.

Madame asked the young man to her room, and told

him quite gently that the spilling of his seed was a sad waste. Then, in the most tender yet casual fashion, she showed the young student how such waste might be avoided.

There was no anxiety, no sense of guilt. The relationship between the student and his generous landlady was simply part of a culture which always stressed the virtue of taking things as they come.

Sexual maturation in the context of such a culture is relatively non-traumatic for both men and women. This may well account for the aura of pleasantness in most French sex jokes and their concentration on adult satisfaction in contrast to the anal-regressive, adolescent, and often cruel sex jokes heard elsewhere.

In England, for example, I was struck by the high proportion of jokes referring to homosexuality. The incestuous component also seems to figure prominently in English jokes, mother-fixations of confirmed bachelors being a standard ingredient.

Oral-genital jokes enjoy high currency in the United States; and we have already touched in Chapter 2 on the American use of anal humor to camouflage class barriers in a supposedly democratic society. The racial antagonisms peculiar to the American environment also find frequent expression in dirty humor.

Regardless of geography, cultural history, or national character, however, all sex jokes have certain factors in common. They are, in effect, highly stylized forms of a four-letter word game—that is, a ploy, a gambit, a mode of adjustment employing obscene terms. The game has multiple goals: seduction, aggression, or release from sexual anxiety, depending on the story and the teller.

For some men, telling a dirty story to a woman is a veiled invitation or a kind of symbolic seduction. Occasionally such men trap women into situations where they are a captive audience, much as men intent on more obvious assault try to get a girl into a corner. Thanks to a certain social sanction surrounding joke-telling—especially at parties and after a few drinks—these men usually get away with making such verbal passes.

Occasionally, however, the obscene raconteur becomes so obtrusive that attempts are made to curb him—always a matter calling for considerable tact, because the man, after all, hasn't "done anything." Once I was asked to conduct a pre-therapeutic interview with a highly respected faculty member of an Eastern college who, unfortunately, used his student-counseling sessions to broaden the humoristic horizons of the coeds. The professor, an exemplar of self-assured urbanity, merely smiled, remarked that a sense of humor doesn't call for psychotherapy, reached for his coat, and bowed out of my office. I do not know what, if any, action was taken by the college administration.

In other respects, however, the telling of dirty stories serves legitimate and altogether salutary functions. The laughter loosed by such jokes provides release from sexual tensions or fears. In doing so, it frees a direct path of communication with our unconscious. Laughter is an instrument on which we play themes that are normally silenced by guilt and fear. Through laughter we are some-

times able to attain grace and ease in the expression of
what otherwise would remain cramped and clandestine.
Through the dirty joke, what oppresses us is transformed
into laughter. And laughter gives us freedom.

Laughter is surely the surest touch of genius in creation.
Would *you* ever have thought of it, I ask you,
If you had been making man, stuffing him full
Of such hopping greeds and passions that he has
To blow himself to pieces as often as he
Conviently can manage it—would it also
Have occurred to you to make him burst himself
With such a phenomenon as cachinnation?
That same laughter . . . almost amounts to revelation.

So writes Christopher Fry, paraphrasing the psychology
of laughter with poetic succinctness. Indeed, laughter
amounts to revelation and therefore release. It is hardly
surprising that Freud soon followed his pioneer work on
dream analysis with the now classic *Jokes and Their Relation to the Unconscious.*

The inner workings of wit, Freud clearly perceived, are
quite similar to those of the dream. Forbidden impulses
are repressed into the subconscious. There thwarted desire is disguised to appear in some other form.

But dream and laughter differ in the method of accom-
plishing this. The dream presents repressed desire as hal-
lucinated wish fulfillment. "In his dreams, the ugliest old
man mounts the fairest maid, and the humble clerk lays
waste the city," observes Heimito von Doderer, the late
Austrian novelist.

171

Wit, by contrast, does not allow the hidden wish to re-appear recognizably. Only the motive is retained: form and concept are changed, imagery and symbols are shifted in the subconscious mind. Finally, the repressed desire emerges as a witty thought. "If this is how Her Majesty treats her prisoners, she doesn't deserve to have any," quips Oscar Wilde of his misery at Reading Gaol. His towering rage at the authority that had imprisoned him, symbolized by the Queen, had been channeled into laughter. Though their methods differ, dream and joke serve the same function: making the unbearable bearable.

In analyzing the dirty joke, we can clearly distinguish numerous categories. There are punning jokes based mainly on double entendre and similar word manipulations. These contrast with conceptual jokes, which refer directly to sexual or excretory parts, acts, or notions. Further subdivisions can be made along psychoanalytic lines among jokes whose principal orientation is oral, anal, or phallic. And one may also establish groupings of jokes dealing with specific problems causing sexual anxiety, such as impotence, castration, incest, abortion.

The dirty joke lets a person deal vicariously (i.e., on the symbolic level) with psychosexual problems which he cannot readily express in any other way. Persons who habitually and compulsively tell dirty jokes are, in essence, externalizing subconscious fears or desires.

When I presented this thought at a lecture some time ago, a member of my audience asked rather testily, "Do you *have* to be Freudian even about a joke?"

I replied that he might as well ask an astronomer

whether he *has* to be Copernican or Keplerian. It is not a matter of arbitrarily choosing interpretations. It is simply a matter of providing a relevant frame for empirical data.

Take, for example, the story about the soldier who had his penis shot off. The field surgeon decided on an organ transplant and grafted the tip of an elephant's trunk onto the soldier's stump. A few weeks later the surgeon asked the soldier how he was getting along. "Fine, sir," came the answer. "No trouble. Except last night. I was at a party and they were passing around peanuts."

The effect of this story would not be nearly the same if it did not touch on nearly universal castration anxieties. True, the image of the amputee reaching for the peanuts at the party is comic, but it is not the real kernel of the story. The laughter is the humorous transformation of a basic fear.

If jokes in print were not invariably dull, I could cite an array of dirty stories documenting every kind of psycho-sexual problem, each joke acting as a release mechanism for a specific type of anxiety. Our concern, however, is not with the joke as such but with its underlying psycho-dynamics. These take their characteristic form quite early in life.

During their pubertal years, many youngsters look to the prospect of sexual intercourse in later years not with anticipatory pleasure but with fear and uncertainty. It appears to them as a threatening demand which they have to fulfill, and they are tormented by doubts about their sexual adequacy. To the adolescent, the dirty joke is a way of shielding himself from these anxieties. For, if you can joke about something, it cannot really be so terrible, after all. In removing some of the fear surrounding sex, the dirty joke is both a healthy and necessary instrument toward sexual adjustment.

In sexually repressive cultures, the dirty joke is often the only permissible way of speaking of sex at all, and joke-swapping sessions among boys—and occasionally also among girls—of high-school age are one of the few ways available to them for releasing sexual tensions and anxieties.

Ultimately, of course, the locker-room joke provides no satisfaction. At best, it is an interim solution to the mounting problem of sexual urgency in adolescence, providing temporary satisfactions of an exhibitionistic or voyeuristic nature. Yet these may afford better preparation for an eventual sexual encounter than the total and basically hypocritical repression nominally demanded in some of our cultural subgroups.

If, however, sexual experience is unduly delayed, the dirty joke no longer functions as a palliative. On the contrary, under conditions of sexual privation it often becomes an irritant that no longer provides release but merely increases expectation. The jokes circulating among men isolated from women, as in the army or in prison, become increasingly desexualized even though they nominally deal with sex. Prolonged frustration turns sexuality into aggression, and many of these jokes, though they refer to the sexual act, become expressions, not of lust but of pure hostility. Usually they are quite crude, blatant, and unfunny.

174

For some men, sex jokes of this sort become a favorite mode of expressing broad, unfocused hostility. A patient of mine, a successful lawyer, would invariably foist the crudest of such jokes upon any social gathering after a few drinks. If anyone attempted to stop him, he was apt to become physically violent. During analysis it developed that these jokes had for him no subjective sexual meaning at all. They were simply a way of lashing out, more or less randomly, at his surroundings.

The same kind of joke—if unfunny crudity can be so called—is also frequently heard among economically exploited groups, to whom oppression is a fact of life as primary and pervasive as sex. To them, the sexual crudity becomes a form of quasi-political protest, a generalized outcry of hate.

The dirty joke, at least in adult life, is an almost exclusively male province. While women, as we noted in the opening chapter, will quite eagerly adopt risqué expressions to flaunt their emancipation, they generally avoid the obscene joke. One possible explanation is that, while a certain four-letter word may be chic and modish, an entire dirty story can't be culturally sanctioned in this way. It can't be institutionalized—it can't become "in" in the way a single word or phrase can.

But this explanation, though quite plausible at a shallow level, fails to touch on the profound difference existing between men and women with respect to obscene humor. This difference far exceeds fashion or a double standard of tolerance. I believe that women generally refrain from telling dirty stories simply because they do not have the psychological need for them that men have.

Reasons for this were suggested by Dr. Martin Grotjahn in his profoundly perceptive study *Beyond Laughter.* "The mature woman smiles tolerantly and pretends to accept the male's false claim to superiority over her. She agrees to accept it because every time the man approaches her sexually, she can show her superiority. She is always ready; he must get ready. She may watch while he must perform. For the man, the sexual act is a test, an examination. If the woman so chooses, she may watch the performance and still perform. The woman is always potentially potent, the man is always potentially impotent. While the woman longs for intercourse, the man performs a kind of 'extracourse.' Where the man discovered love through sex, the woman discovered sex through love." With all these psychologic advantages—at least during maturity—woman needs no reassurance from dirty stories, no bolstering through obscenity.

The fact that women rarely tell dirty jokes does not mean that they fail to appreciate their humor. In fact, as Grotjahn observes, women have a better chance of attaining a true sense of humor than have men. For mature humor is based on a firm sense of reality, and, to quote again, "Woman needs illusion only until she recognizes her strength. The woman's calm, realistic self-reliance is [in] striking contrast to the man's tense, alert search for self-assurance."

Yet, despite these sex differences, it is in the realm of humor that a man and woman can attain the most fruitful ground for a deepening relationship. For at the level of adult maturity, humor—sexual or otherwise—blends into a wider emotional realm to which both men and women gain entry through sublimation and through love. Extending far beyond the concept of the "funny," it encompasses broad life adjustments in an aura of shared laughter. As Grotjahn so poetically phrases it: "Laughter is a way of anxiety-free communication with our unconscious to keep our imagination and intuition alive; to create freely; to form our life. With such rebirth, experienced without guilt, fear, or anxiety, performed with grace and with ease . . . we become essentially and incurably human."

Conclusion

Verbal obscenity is undoubtedly a universal phenomenon. If it did not exist in all known languages, it would probably have to be invented in order to permit humans a psychologically suitable vehicle for the ventilation of fury and despair, the elimination of anger and aggression, the expression of rebellion, and the suppression of fears.

Psychoanalytical research and observation have established many of the meanings and aims of obscene language in daily life. Anthropological, philological, and sociological research have brought forward additional invaluable insights. One of the most fascinating works relating to this field has been the study of obscene language-usage in certain types of interpersonal transactions which Eric Berne, in his book *Games People Play*, calls "games." According to his definition, a game is a "recurrent set of transactions with a concealed motivation," thus differentiated from procedures, rituals, pastimes, and operations. "Every game," he states, "is basically dishonest," because it is based upon gimmicky maneuvers designed to arrive at a "pay-off" or a "killing."

The FLWGs which I have described and analyzed in these pages do have ulterior aims: omnipotence, aggressive self-assertion, displacement of anxiety, narcissistic prestige, and sexual power. They too are devised to attack, offend, mislead, punish, excite, or seduce—intentionally, magically, or compulsively. They may occur in real life as well as in dreams and daytime fantasies. They may be used by creeps, jerks, goons, queers, pimps, desperados, intellectuals, mental defectives, psychotics, soldiers, sailors, dentists, and headshrinkers. As a matter of fact, nearly everybody uses these FLWGs, at least occasionally. Some people play these games sneakily, in an inaudible form. They keep their obscene thoughts to themselves.

FLWGs seem to be particularly important and essential to grievance-collectors, semanticists, post-pubertal pseudo-adults, conventional hipsters and eccentrics, anatomically oriented dramatists, pussyfooting poets, iconoclastic heroes, and disillusioned ex-priests. Their often radical, superlative, paradoxical, and exotic colorfulness produces affective impacts and consequences which ordinary word games can never hope to achieve.

The communicative value of such FLWGs can certainly not be underestimated, inasmuch as four-letter words, in spite of their often hidden meanings, possess a distinct directness and superior effectiveness which, though they may lead to misgivings, do not give rise to misunderstandings. Their relationship to humor is historically incontestable, although frequently anti-pastoral, dead-panicky, fetichistic, psycho-massacrous and subversive.

FLWGs are most colorful, off-color interpersonal operations which transform the unspeakable into a natural idiom of anti-value and rebellion against the most staggering dogmatic and psychosclerotic conventionalities of everyday life. They have to be studied in order to be understood as signs of health as well as symptoms of pathology in the human search for individual and cultural identity.

Bibliography

Abse, David W., "Psychodynamic Aspects of the Problem of Definition of Obscenity," *Contemporary Problems of Law*, Vol. 20, 1955, pp. 572-582.

Bergler, Edmund, "On Obscene Words," *Psychoanalytic Quarterly*, Vol. 5, 1936, pp. 246-248.

Bettelheim, Bruno, *Symbolic Wounds* (Puberty Rites and the Envious Male) Collier Books, New York, 1962.

Cary, H.N., *Introduction to Sexual Vocabulary*, 2 vols., unpublished, Chicago, 1920, typescript at the Institute for Sex Research, Inc., Bloomington, Ind.

———, *Sexual Vocabulary*, 5 vols., unpublished, not dated (ca. 1916), typescript at Institute for Sex Research, Inc., Bloomington, Ind.

Diamond, A.S., *The History and Origin of Language*, Philosophical Society, New York, 1959.

Ellis, Albert, *The American Sexual Tragedy*, Lyle Stuart, New York, 1962.

——— and Abarbanel, Albert (editors) *The Encyclopedia of Sexual Behavior*, Hawthorn Books, New York, 1961.

Ellis, Havelock, *The Revaluation of Obscenity*, Hours Press, Paris, 1931 (reprinted in *More Essays on Love and Virtue*, Doubleday, Doran, New York, 1931).

Evans-Pritchard, E.E., "Some Collective Expressions of Obscenity in Africa," *Journal of the Royal Anthropological Institute of Great Britain and Ireland,* 59, 1929, pp. 311-331.

Feldman, Marvin J., "The Use of Obscene Words in the Therapeutic Relationship," *The American Journal of Psychoanalysis,* Vol. XV, No. 1, 1955.

Ferenczi, Sandor, *Sex in Psychoanalysis,* Basic Books, New York, 1950.

Fitch, Robert E., "La Mystique de la Merde," *New Republic,* Sept. 3, 1956, p. 17.

Freud, Sigmund, *Jokes and Their Relation to the Unconscious,* W.W. Norton & Co., New York, 1960.

Gehner, L.E., *Erotic Aspects of Chinese Culture,* Washington, privately printed, 1957.

—— *Erotic Aspects of Japanese Culture,* Washington, privately printed, 1953.

Goldman, Albert, "The Comedy of Lenny Bruce," *Commentary,* October 1963.

Graves, Robert, *Lars Porsena or the Future of Swearing and Improper Language,* Dutton, New York, 1927.

Grotjahn, Martin, *Beyond Laughter,* Blakiston Division, McGraw-Hill Book Co., Inc., New York, 1957.

Herman, Imré, "The Giant Mother, the Phallic Mother, Obscenity," *Psychoanalytic Review,* Vol. 36, 1949.

Howland, A.H., "Boshesh or Kadesh? A Study into the Sources of Obscene Ideas About Obscenity," Journal of Sexol. Psychoanalysis, Vol. 1, 1923, pp. 289-296.

Joffe, Natalie F., "The Vernacular of Menstruation," *Word 4,* Dec. 1948, pp. 181-186.

Johnson, Burges, "Modern Maledictions, Execrations and Cusswords," *North American Review,* 238, November 1934,, pp. 467-471.

——, "The Everyday Profanity of Our Best People," *Century Magazine*, 92, June 1916, pp. 311-314.

Johnson, Falk, "The History of Some Dirty Words," *American Mercury*, 71, November 1950, pp. 538-545.

Jones, E., "A Linguistic Factor in English Characterology," *International Journal of Psychoanalysis*, 1920, Vol. 1, p. 256.

Junod, Henri Alexandre, *The Life of a South African Tribe*, 2nd ed. Macmillan, London, 1927.

Justinian, *Americana Sexualis*, privately printed, Chicago, 1939.

Kaplan, Abraham, "Obscenity as an Aesthetic Category," in Hook, S., *American Philosophers at Work*, Criterion Books, New York, 1956, pp. 397-417.

Kinsey, Pomeroy, Martin and Gebhard, *Sexual Behavior in the Human Female*, W.B. Saunders Co., Philadelphia and London, 1953.

——, *Sexual Behavior in the Human Male*, W.B. Saunders Co., Philadelphia and London, 1948.

Kronhausen, Eberhard and Phyllis, *Pornography and the Law* (The Psychology of Erotic Realism and Pornography), Ballantine Books, New York, 1959.

LaBarre, Weston, "Obscenity: An Anthropological Appraisal," *Law and Contemporary Problems*, 20, Autumn 1955, pp. 533-543.

McDougald, Duncan, Jr., "Language and Sex," *The Encyclopedia of Sexual Behavior*, Hawthorn Books, New York, 1961.

Malinowski, Bronislaw, *Sex and Repression in Savage Society*, Meridian Books, New York, 1955.

Marcus, Steven, *The Other Victorians—A Study of Sexuality and Pornography in Mid-Nineteenth Century England*, Basic Books, New York, 1966.

Meredith, Mamie, "Inexpressibles, Unmentionables, Unwhisperables, and Other Verbal Delicacies of the Mid-Nineteenth Century Americans," *American Speech,* 5, April 1930, pp. 285-287.

Read, Allen Walker, "An Obscenity Symbol," *American Speech,* 9, December 1934, pp. 264-278.

Roberts, Edwin A., Jr., *The Smut Rakers,* Newsbook, The National Observer, Silver Springs, 1966.

Sagarin, Edward, *The Anatomy of Dirty Words,* Lyle Stuart, New York, 1962.

Sapir, Edward, *Culture, Language and Personality,* University of California Press, Berkeley and Los Angeles, 1960.

Steadman, John Marcellus, "A Study of Verbal Taboos," *American Speech,* 10, April 1935, pp. 93-103.

Stone, Leo, "On the Principal Obscene Word of the English Language," *International Journal of Psychoanalysis,* Vol. XXXV, 1954, pp. 30-56.

Woolf, H.B., *The G.I.'s Favorite Four-Letter Word,* privately printed, Baton Rouge, La., 1948.

Young, Wayland, *Eros Denied* (Sex in Western Society), Grove Press, New York, 1966.

About the Authors

RENATUS HARTOGS, M.D., PH.D. comes from an old Dutch family. He received his medical degrees in Brussels and Montreal and his Ph.D. degree in psychology as well as his psychoanalytical training in Germany. He came to the United States late in 1940.

Dr. Hartogs is Chief Psychiatrist of Youth House and the New York Detention House for Juvenile Delinquents and Medical Director of Community Guidance Service of New York City. His previous books are *How to Grow Up Successfully* and *The Two Assassins*.

HANS FANTEL is Viennese by birth. As a professional writer he has worked in several fields. In addition to scientific reporting, Mr. Fantel writes about music and is an expert on the subject of high fidelity. He makes his home in New York City.